# 100 DAYS
## IN THE SECRET PLACE

*Gene Edwards*

**Destiny Image® Publishers, Inc.**
**P.O. Box 310**
**Shippensburg, PA 17257-0310**

"Speaking to the Purposes of God for This
Generation and for the Generations to Come"

ISBN 0-7684-2065-2

For Worldwide Distribution
Printed in the U.S.A.

Second Printing: 2002          Third Printing: 2002

This book and all other Destiny Image, Revival Press, MercyPlace,
Fresh Bread, Destiny Image Fiction, and Treasure House books are available
at Christian bookstores and distributors worldwide.

For a U.S. bookstore nearest you, call **1-800-722-6774**.
For more information on foreign distributors, call **717-532-3040**.
Or reach us on the Internet:
**www.destinyimage.com**

# Contents

# Introduction

On very rare occasions a generation will produce a number of great Christians. Perhaps the only time in Church history when *four* such people came to prominence was in the late 1600s. One was Jeanne Guyon, whose writings are revered and read today more than ever before. The second was a friend of hers, the Archbishop Fenelon of France. The third is the only person whose writings are almost as popular as Jeanne Guyon. He was a simple servant in the Carmelite Order of monks. His name was Brother Lawrence. He and Jeanne Guyon were contemporaries, both living in France at the same time, though they never met.* The fourth man is not as well-known today. However, he was better known, in his lifetime, than the other three combined. His name is Michael Molinos. He died sealed in a prison dungeon in Rome. His book *The Spiritual Guide* has been virtually forgotten, having been only recently resurrected. The quality of this book is without challenge.

Here then is a brief look at the lives of the three whose writings are in this devotional book.

* The works of Brother Lawrence survive as letters to friends. If you would like to read those letters see *Practicing His Presence* by Brother Lawrence, SeedSowers Publishing House; Jacksonville, FL.

# BIOGRAPHIES

# FRANÇOIS DE FENELON

There are a few Christians who have been revered almost from the moment they arrived on the scene. One such man is François de Fenelon.

Even today, in French history, he is honored as one of the most godly, saintly men to ever walk across the stage of Roman Catholic history. He rose quickly to the status of bishop, and then to Archbishop. At the time when the Huguenots (French Protestants) were forced out of France, the king gave Fenelon the responsibility of instructing those Protestants who were willing to come into the Catholic Church. He was also given charge of the grandson of Louis XIV, to train this heir to the throne, in a spiritual walk with Jesus Christ. (Unfortunately, this promising young man died while still in his youth.) There came a moment in French history when an entire nation was focused on three people: two Archbishops, Fenelon and Bossuet, and Jeanne Guyon. The two Archbishops were arguing over the teachings of Jeanne Guyon. Try to imagine two Roman Catholic Archbishops in the late 1600s publicly dueling over a woman. Had such an event happened in our day, it would have headlined every newspaper and been the lead story on every radio and television news broadcast. Nothing like this had ever happened before The question was very simple: Was Jeanne Guyon a heretic? Or, was she one of the great spiritual voices of the Catholic Church?

Later, after Guyon disappeared into the Bastille, Fenelon's letters emerged as unparalleled in their spiritual depth. These letters have never gone out of print; his life and his writings have been unassailable.

During the late 1600s Bossuet was considered the Martin Luther of the Catholic Church—he was more famous than any other of his day. Today his name is almost lost in oblivion.

Between the writings of Guyon and Fenelon you will find the richest spiritual treasures afforded to you today.

Fenelon died in 1715 as a result of an accident that befell him while riding a carriage across a bridge.

The deaths of Guyon and Fenelon brought to a close an epic, not only in French history, but also in Christian history. Since then no voices have arisen to take believers to the heights of spiritual riches, as have they.

# MICHAEL MOLINOS

Everything about Michael Molinos seems to be a tragedy. Yet we need to remember that at one time Michael Molinos was revered in the Catholic Church as much as its two greatest illuminaries, Saint Teresa and John of the Cross, both of Spain.

Is it a coincidence that Michael Molinos was also born in Spain about one hundred years after John of the Cross and Saint Teresa?

As a young man Molinos was brought to the Vatican in Rome. He became one of the most influential people there, then Italy and throughout Europe! Thousands were drawn to his ministry. It is said that at one time 20,000 people in Naples were in home meetings following his *Spiritual Guide*. The Order of the Jesuits became quite fearful and jealous of him. Charges were made against him. The charges were found to be baseless and his influence grew. Later his books found their way into every language in Western Europe. Some have speculated that his Spiritual Guide influenced Jeanne Guyon. This is almost certainly not true; nonetheless, history refers to both of them as Quietist: both taught that being quiet before God and in the presence of persecution was God's will. Another way to describe what they taught is that Christians should be indifferent to the negative things that befall them.

The Jesuits tried again to ruin Molinos. He was finally forced into a trial in 1687. Molinos was found guilty of heresy. All over Europe his books were burned. Further, *The Spiritual Guide* was put on the Vatican's blacklist. If a man dared even possess the book it meant automatic excommunication from the Church.

Molinos was sealed in a dungeon and his face never seen again. He died in 1696. Nonetheless, there was a story that while in the dungeon he did "repent" of his teaching. The Pope declared a holiday in Rome. People danced in the streets upon hearing that "the great heretic" had relented. In the vault where he is laid, the only words written thereon are: "Michael Molinos—The Great Heretic."

Molinos was tried in secret. The transcript of that trial has never been released. To this day it is kept under lock and key. The Vatican refuses to give access of the transcripts to anyone. It appears that having a close walk with the Lord is not religiously acceptable. Perhaps the only thing that has kept the knowledge of Michael Molinos alive is the charge that Jeanne Guyon was one of his students.

His monumental work, *The Spiritual Guide*, has only recently been put back into print.

The works of Guyon, Fenelon, and Molinos bear striking resemblance in many ways. Perhaps the most unique aspect of this similarity is the fact that they were all so practical.

There is a great deal of spiritual verbiage, but you can usually note that such writers rarely get practical. These three knew the problems we face as we attempt to walk closely with the Lord Jesus Christ. All three also offered solutions to our problems. Their lives also reflect what they taught. All three had that rare willingness to go to the cross, to neither attack nor defend.

You now have in your possession one hundred pages of their writings. You can find no better literature in the English language to point you to the Lord and His ways. May these three witnesses join as one voice to speak to your life.

# JEANNE GUYON

Few people are aware of the incredible influence Jeanne Guyon has had on the Christian family for the last three hundred years, more so than some who have founded denominations, and perhaps *all* of the great and famous names of Christian history. Only one author, from the century in which she lived, outsells her. His name is William Shakespeare. In fact, they are the only two writers of the 1600s whose books are still *very* popular.

Jeanne Guyon is the most read woman in Christian history. Even now her influence covers the globe. Her books have been published in all major languages. No one has ever written with the depth that this woman has. Her words are to be taken to heart and cherished. She is a Christian author without parallel.

Jeanne Guyon was born in 1648. By the time she reached the age of thirty she was one of the most influential Christians in France. Nonetheless, it seems she could not stay out of trouble with the Catholic Church. She was imprisoned in the nunnery of Anthony even before she was well-known! She was later arrested on several occasions. Those arrests were based more on the jealousies and intrigues within the court of Louis XIV than anything about her writings or her life. Guyon was finally forced to stand before a tribunal of inquiry. She was judged on her biography and her books *The Song of Songs* and *Spiritual Torrents*. Two of the three bishops on the tribunal moved to set her free, thereby forcing the third, Archbishop Bossuet, to agree. Nonetheless, Bossuet tricked her into leaving his dioceses saying that she did so without his permission. Louis XIV hated this woman and had her arrested on this pretext.

As punishment, she was first interned in the tower of Vincenne and later transferred to the Bastille.

Guyon's autobiography, which was written for private inspection, has become one of the greatest biographies in Christian history.

You will not find any writer of any generation who has reached the depths that she has reached. Read her and read her well. She is the best that the Christian faith has to offer, especially for those looking for a deeper walk with Christ.

# WAY OF THE CROSS

# EMBRACING THE CROSS

You need to learn to separate yourself from unnecessary and restless thoughts which grow out of self-love. When your own thoughts are set aside you will be completely in the middle of the straight and narrow path. You will experience the freedom and peace that is meant for you as a child of God.

I try to follow the same advice that I give others. I know that I must seek peace in the same way. Often, when you suffer, it is the life of your self-nature that causes you pain. When you are dead you do not suffer. If you were completely dead to your old nature you would no longer feel many of the pains that now bother you.

Endure the aches and pains of your body with patience. Do the same thing with your spiritual afflictions (that is, trouble sent to you that you cannot control). Do not add to the cross in your life by becoming so busy that you have no time to sit quietly before God. Do not resist what God brings into your life. Be willing to suffer if that is what is needed. Over-activity and stubbornness will only increase your anguish.

God prepares a cross for you that you must embrace without thought of self-preservation. The cross is painful. Accept the cross and you will find peace even in the middle of turmoil. Let me warn you that if you push the cross away, your circumstances will become twice as hard to bear. In the long run, the pain of resisting the cross is harder to live with than the cross itself.

See God's hand in the circumstances of your life. Do you want to experience true happiness? Submit yourself peacefully and simply to the will of God, and bear your sufferings without struggle. Nothing so shortens and soothes your pain as the spirit of non-resistance to your Lord.

As wonderful as this sounds, it still may not stop you from bargaining with God. The hardest thing about suffering is not knowing how great it will be or how long it will last. You will be tempted to want to impose some limits to your suffering. No doubt you will want to control the intensity of your pain.

Do you see the stubborn and hidden hold you have over your life? This control makes the cross necessary in the first place. Do not reject the full work that the power of the cross could accomplish in you. Unfortunately, you will be forced to go over the same ground again and again. Worse yet, you will suffer much, but your suffering will be for no purpose.

May the Lord deliver you from falling into an inner state in which the cross is not at work in you! God loves a cheerful giver. (See Second Corinthians 9:7.) Imagine how much He must love those who abandon themselves to His will cheerfully and completely—even if it results in their crucifixion!

—FENELON

## The Cross—A Bond of Love

I am sorry to hear of your troubles, but I am sure you realize that you must carry the cross with Christ in this life. Soon enough there will come a time when you will no longer suffer. You will reign with God and He will wipe away your tears with His own hand. In His presence, pain and sighing will forever flee away.

So while you have the opportunity to experience difficult trials, do not lose the slightest opportunity to embrace the cross. Learn to suffer in humility and in peace. Your deep self-love makes the cross too heavy to bear. Learn to suffer with simplicity and a heart full of love. If you do you will not only be happy in spite of the cross, but because of it. Love is pleased to suffer for the Well-Beloved. The cross which conforms you into His image is a consoling bond of love between you and Him.

—Fenelon

## Trust Your Self-Love to God

I have no doubt that God treats you as one of His friends by giving you the cross. God's way accomplishes His purpose quicker than anything you could think of. God is able to seek out and destroy the roots of self-love. You, on your own, could never find those hidden roots. God can see the entire path of self-love within your heart. Let Him attack self-love at its strongest point.

Pray for strength and faith enough to trust yourself completely to God. Follow Him simply wherever He may lead you and you will not have to think up big plans to bring about your perfection. Your new life will begin to grow naturally.

I know you want to see the road ahead rather than trusting God. If you continue this way, the road will get longer and your spiritual progress will slow down. Give yourself as completely as you can to God. Do so until your final breath, and He will never desert you.

—FENELON

# THE PATH OF CHRIST

God will eventually test you in all areas of your life, but He will not let your trials become greater than you can bear. Let God use trials to help you grow. Do not try to measure your progress, your strength, or what God is doing. His work is not less efficient because what He is doing is invisible. Much of God's work is done in secret because you would not die to yourself if He always visibly stretched out His hand to save you. God does not transform you on a bed of light, life, and grace. His transformation is done on the cross in darkness, poverty, and death.

What valid questions do you have about the truth of Christianity? You really fear having to submit to someone beside yourself. You also fear having to walk the difficult road toward becoming conformed to the image of Christ. You see clearly the sacrifices you will have to make to follow Christ completely and you are shrinking back.

Christ did not say, "If anyone will come after me, let him enjoy himself, let him be gorgeously dressed, let him be drunk with delight." He never even said, "Be glad that you are perfect and that you can see how well you are doing." No, Jesus said, "If anyone will come after me, let him deny himself, take up his cross and follow me." His path winds up the side of a steep mountain where death will be present on every hand. (See Matthew 16:24.)

You do not yet see the lovely side of following Christ. You see what He takes away, but you do not see what He gives. You exaggerate the sacrifices and ignore the blessings.

Paul tells you that you desire to be clothed, but it is necessary that you be stripped before you can put on Christ. Allow Him to strip your self-love of every covering so that you might receive the white robe washed in the blood of the Lamb. You need only His purity.

Listen to what I have to say. It is not easy to hear, but it will feed your spirit. Do not listen to the voice that suggests that you live for yourself. The voice of self-love is even more powerful than the voice of the serpent. If the world never asked for anything more than what you could give out of love, wouldn't it be a better master?

Christ leaves no emptiness within you. You will be led to do things which you will find enjoyable, and you will like them better than doing all the things which have led you astray. How happy you will be when you do not possess anything of your own but give yourself completely to your Lord. Bride of Jesus, how beautiful you are when you no longer have anything of your own, but seek only His beauty. You will then be the delight of your Bridegroom, and He will be all your beauty! He will love you without measure. He will put His own life in you.

—FENELON

# THE WAYS OF GOD

When God starts to deal with your old nature He heads straight for the center of all that you hold most dear. Allow Him to bring you the cross in the very center of who you are. Don't grumble and become agitated when the process starts: Silence and peace will help you much more than being upset.

You will be tempted to speak out in a humble tone of voice to tell others of your problems. Watch out for this! A humility that is still talkative does not run very deep. When you talk too much your self-love relieves its sense of shame a little.

Don't be angry about what people say. Just follow God and let them talk. As far as people are concerned, you will never be able to satisfy them. Silence, peace, and union with God should comfort you from all that people speak against you. You need to be determined to do right in your present situation—but at the same time your quick temper requires checks and balances. Come to God often just to sit in His presence and renew yourself. Nothing is as important as lowliness of heart, and detachment from your own opinion and will. Stiffness and harshness is not the spirit of Jesus Christ.

—FENELON

# TAKE UP YOUR CROSS

To bear the cross simply, without letting your self-love add all sorts of dilemmas to it, will make your life easier.

When you accept the cross and simply allow it to do the work God intended, you will be happy because you will see what good fruit is produced in you.

When you love God, it will not matter to you what you must suffer on His behalf. The cross will make you over in the image of your Beloved. Here is real consolation—a true bond of love.

You are bearing the burden of some old ones who can no longer bear their own. Reason weakens at so old an age. Goodness, unless deeply rooted, lessens. All the strength seems to go to the temper! Accept and welcome this burden as the cross.

It is a blessing that you have some free hours to rest in peace in the bosom of the Lord. This is where you will refresh yourself and gain strength to go on. Take care of your health and try to take some time to rest and enjoy yourself. As others grow older you should expect less and less of them. Don't expect too much of yourself, either.

—Fenelon

# The Hidden Cross

God has all sorts of circumstances to bring you the cross, and they all accomplish His purpose. He may even join physical weakness to your emotional and spiritual suffering. Of course the world may not see you dealing with the cross—they think you are just touchy or prone to fits of nervous exhaustion. So while you are bent double under the hidden work of the cross, onlookers often envy your apparent good fortune.

What do you say to God when you are under the work of the cross? You need not say a lot to Him, or even think of Him much. He sees your suffering, and your willingness to submit. With people you love you do not need to continually say, "I love you with all my heart." Even if you do not think about how much you love Him, you still love God every bit as much. True love is deep down in the spirit—simple, peaceful, and silent.

How do you bear suffering? Silently before God. Do not disturb yourself by trying to manufacture an artificial sense of God's presence. Slowly you will learn that all the troubles in your life—your job, your health, your inward failings—are really cures to the poison of your old nature. Learn to bear these sufferings in patience and meekness.

—FENELON

## THE VALUE OF THE CROSS

Do you wonder why God has to make it so hard on you? Why doesn't He make you good without making you miserable in the meantime? Of course He could, but He does not choose to do so. He wants you to grow a little at a time and not burst into instant maturity. This is what He has decided and you can only adore His wisdom—even when you don't understand it.

I am awed by what suffering can produce. You and I are nothing without the cross. I agonize and cry when the cross is working within me, but when it is over I look back in admiration for what God has accomplished. Of course I am then ashamed that I bore it so poorly. I have learned so much from my foolish reactions.

You yourself must endure the painful process of change. There is much more at work here than your instant maturity. God wants to build a relationship with you that is based on faith and trust and not on glamorous miracles.

God uses the disappointments, disillusionments, and failures of your life to take your trust away from yourself and help you put your trust in Him. It is like being burned in a slow fire, but you would rather be burned up in a blaze of glory, wouldn't you? How would this fast burn detach you from yourself? Thus God prepares events to detach you from yourself and from others.

God is your Father, do you think He would ever hurt you? He just cuts you off from those things you love in the wrong way. You cry like a baby when God removes something or someone from your life, but you would cry a lot more if you saw the eternal harm your wrong attachments cause you.

You do not see with the eyes of eternity. God knows everything. Nothing happens without His consent. You are upset by small losses, but do not see eternal gains! Don't dwell on your suffering. Your oversensitivity makes your trials worse. Abandon yourself to God.

Everything in you that is not already a part of the established kingdom of God needs the cross. When you accept the cross in love, His kingdom begins to come to life within you. You must bear the cross and be satisfied with what pleases God. You have need of the cross. The faithful Giver of every good gift gives the cross to you with His own hand. I pray you will come to see how blessed it is to be corrected for your own good.

My God, help us to see Jesus as our model in all suffering. You nailed Him to the cross for us. You made Him a man of sorrows to teach us how useful sorrow is. Give us a heart to turn our backs on ourselves and trust only in You.

—FENELON

# A VIOLENT KINGDOM

Whom do you think Paul was talking to when he said, "We are fools for the sake of Jesus Christ, and you are wise in Jesus Christ." To you! Not to the people who do not know God! He is talking to all who think they can work out their own salvation without accepting the folly of the cross of Jesus. No one wants to be humiliated and put down. It is not something to be excited about, but it is the way of God.

You cannot give place to the world, to your passions or your laziness. Words are not enough to claim the kingdom of God. It takes strength and courage and violence. You must violently resist the tides of the world. Violently give up all that holds you back from God. Violently turn your will over to God to do His will alone.

This violence is what I pray you will come to know, for how else will you know anything of the life of the Lord Jesus?

—FENELON

# THE SACRIFICE OF LOVE

If you follow God only to feel His presence and comfort, then you follow Him for the wrong reasons. Your mind is anxious to know, your heart wants to feel sweet feelings, but you are not willing to follow Christ to the cross. Is this dying to self?

There is refined spiritual ambition in unduly pursuing spiritual gifts. Paul speaks of a better way. "Love does not seek her own." How will you go on to maturity if you are always seeking the consolation of feeling the presence of God with you? To seek pleasure and to ignore the cross will not get you very far. You will soon be trapped in the pursuit of spiritual pleasures.

If you have too tender a childhood in Jesus Christ, you will be in for a hard time when God starts to wean you away from the sensed comfort of God's presence. Don't live on the porch and think you are in the house! The beginnings of your faith may be accompanied by many wonderful feelings, but this does not mean you are mature. Hold to God alone and do not rely on anything you feel or taste or imagine. You will come to see how much safer this way is than chasing after visions and prophesies.

# THE PURPOSE OF SUFFERING

God never makes you suffer unnecessarily. He intends for your suffering to heal and purify you. The hand of God hurts you as little as it can.

Anxiety brings suffering. Sometimes you are simply unwilling to suffer, and you end up resisting God's work. If you put away all your restless longings and your anxiety, you will experience the peace and freedom that God gives to His children. The yoke that God gives is easy to bear if you accept it without struggling to escape. You make life more painful for yourself when you resist God in the least way.

Usually you bargain with God to set a limit on your suffering. The same inward waywardness that makes the work of the cross necessary in your life is what will try to push the cross away. God has to start over with you every time you push Him away.

Sometimes God takes away His gifts until you can possess them purely. Otherwise, they will poison you. It is rare to hold God's gifts without possessiveness. You think everything is for you. You do not think first of the glory of God or you would not become depressed when your visible blessings vanish. The truth is, you are mostly concerned with yourself. Self-love is proud of its spiritual accomplishments. You must lose everything to find God for Himself alone. But you won't lose everything until it is ripped from you. You won't begin to let go of yourself until you have been thrown off a cliff! He takes away to give back in a better way.

Look at the example of friendships. At first God attracts you by pouring His presence out on you. You are eager to pray and to turn away from your selfish comforts and friendships. You give up everyone and everything that does not feel the same as you do. Many people never get past this place. Some get past this to letting God strip them of everything, but get depressed when everything becomes a burden. Far from looking for friends, the friends they used to enjoy now irritate them. Here is agony and despair. Joy cannot be found.

Does this surprise you? God takes everything because you do not know how to love, so do not speak of friendship. The very idea brings tears to your eyes. Everything overcomes you. You do not know what you want. You are moody and cry like a child. You are a mass of swirling emotions which change from moment to moment. Do you find it hard to believe that a strong and high-minded person can be reduced to such a state? To speak of friendship is like speaking of dancing to a sick person.

Wait until the winter is past. Your true friends will come back to you. You will no longer love for yourself, but in and for God. Before, you were somehow always afraid of losing— no matter how generous you appeared. If you didn't seek wealth or honor, you sought common interest or confidence or understanding.

Take away these comforts and you are pained, hurt, and offended. Doesn't this show who you really love?

When it is God you love in someone, you stand by that person no matter what. If the friendship is broken in the order of God, you are at peace. You may feel a deep pain, for the friendship was a great gift, but it is a calm suffering, and free from the cutting grief of a possessive love. God's love sets you free.

Do not waste your suffering. Let suffering accomplish what God wants it to in your life. Never get so hard that you suffer for no reason and for no purpose. Paul says, "God loves a cheerful giver." How much He must love those who cheerfully give themselves to His dealings.

—FENELON

# Two Kinds of Darkness

And now we come to another set of twos. There are two kinds of darkness, an unhappy darkness and a happy darkness.

The first darkness is that which arises from sin. It is a darkness that is filled with unhappiness and leads the Christian to eternal death. The second kind of darkness is darkness which the Lord allows within our inward part in order to establish and settle virtue. This is a happy darkness because it illuminates your inward spirit, strengthens it and gives it greater light.

Consequently, you ought *not* to be grieved and upset when your way is obscure and there is darkness around you. Nor are you to suppose you are lacking in the presence of God, that He has left you or does not love you. Further, the light you formerly possessed must not be seen as some great loss; nor the former relationship you had with the Lord—no matter how blessed it was and no matter that it has totally ceased to exist—as a great loss. It is not.

I would have you see these times of darkness as a happy darkness, a darkness in which you should persevere in your inward pursuit. It is a manifest sign that God, in His infinite mercy, is seeking to bring you into the inward path. How good will be the results, dear friend, if you will but simply embrace these times with peace and with resignation! Such times are for your spiritual good. These times of darkness *do not* slow you down in your journey toward Him! They may seem to, but in fact they hasten you toward the final point of your journey.

—MOLINOS

## LOSS OF SPIRITUAL INTEREST

Perhaps it will be your experience that soon after you have decided to die to a more external life and have moved toward His high mountain you will feel as though nothing is working in your favor! All the wonderful experiences you cherish will dry up. You will hardly be able to discuss spiritual things, or perhaps you will find you have gone so far as to not be able to conceive a good thought of God. Heaven will seem to have turned to brass and there will be little, if any, light. And when you turn back to concentration and thinking, even your thoughts will not be able to comfort you.

Be sure that, if this is the case in your life, your enemy will come to you with suggestion, unclean thoughts, impatience, pride, rage, cursing, confusion and much more. Perhaps you will even feel a distaste for the things of God. And you will feel you have lost some of the keenness of your spiritual understanding. Some will go so far as to feel there is no God, at least no God for them. You will wonder if you have even one good desire left in you.

Do not be afraid. These times and these things have a purging effect. You will grow in a sense of your own unworthiness, and in a realization of the need for your outward appetites to be dealt with. Only the Lord can cast the Jonah of your outward senses into the sea. Be sure that all of your strivings and thrashings are going to be worthless. Any external efforts of piety, or religion, or even of self denial, will *not* work. Rather, such things will aid in shining light upon you, a light that says, "You can do nothing. *All things* are in His hands and not in yours."

—MOLINOS

# CIRCUMSTANCES

It is the nature of each of us to be rather base, proud, ambitious, full of a great deal of appetite, judgments, rationalizations, and opinions. If something does not come into our lives to humiliate us then surely all these things will undo us.

So, what does your Lord do? He allows your faith to be assaulted, even with suggestions of pride, gluttony, rage, perhaps blaspheming, cursing and yes, even despair. All of these serve to humble our natural pride, as a wholesome medicine within the midst of these assaults.

You know that Isaiah reminds us all that righteousness is just so many smelly rags—and that in spite of all our vanity, conceit, and self love.

Your Lord desires to purify your soul, and He can use a very rough file. Yes, He may even assault the purer and nobler things of your life! These assaults serve as a revelation to awaken the human soul…for the soul to *truly* discover, to truly know, just how miserable is its natural state.

And, if you seek spiritual counsel from someone during such times, it is possible that you may receive some help…but you would be very wise not to *expect* help. Deep within you is a place of internal peace, and if you are to come through these periods and if you are not to lose that peace it is necessary for you to believe. You must believe in the fineness of Divine mercy...even when that mercy humbles, afflicts and tries you. How happy you will be if you will simply be quiet before the Lord! Even if these times are caused by the devil, you are nonetheless in the sovereign hand of God, and these things will turn out for your gain and your spiritual profit.

—MOLINOS

# TEMPTATION

I would say that the greatest temptation is to be without temptations. The greatest onslaught is to be without any onslaught at all. Therefore be glad when you are assaulted. With resignation, peace and consistency...abide. There, in internal regions, walk and live.

You must walk the path of temptation. You will not walk down this road very far before you discover that the most internal parts of you (at least those which you can find) are scattered. Scattered and active, moving from one thing to another. There is a great deal of busyness down there!

How can you collect these many and divergent things that are happening within you?

Your Lord calls them together by *faith* and by *silence*, in the presence of God. Collect yourself in His presence with the one purpose and intent of loving Him. Come to Him as one who is giving himself to God. Behold Him in the most inward recess of your spirit that you can find. Do not employ imagination. Rest in love and come to Him in a general way of love and faith, coming for no specific claim, request or desire.

—MOLINOS

# FIRMNESS IN PRAYER

The consistency of true prayer is in *faith*, and in *waiting* on Him. First you *believe* that you are in His presence. You *believe* that you are turning to Him with your heart. And you wait there before Him, tranquilly. These are the only preparations that you need. The *final* results contain a great deal of fruit.

You may expect the enemy to come to you, to disquiet you and cause you trouble, for that is his nature. You will find that the nature of those things you have always enjoyed—pleasures your outward senses have derived from spiritual things (including areas in which you are gifted)—all these will become weak.

You might even expect weariness. All exercise can become difficult. Whether you have these, or other problems...persevere!

You can expect to suffer through problems of a multitude of thoughts, problems of the imagination, provocation of your natural desires, and problems of an inward life that is very dry. All of these temptations must yield to the spirit.

Though these situations are all referred to as *dryness*, truthfully they are very profitable. That is, they are profitable if you embrace them and receive them with patience.

And if it seems to you that you have done nothing in the time that you have set aside for the Lord, do not be deceived. A good heart—a firmness in prayer—is something that is very pleasing to your Lord.

When we come to the Lord in this way we labor *without* personal interest. We labor merely for the glory of God. Surely it may seem that we wait in vain, yet this is not so. We are as the young men who work in the field with their father. At the end of the day, unlike the hired labor, we receive no pay.

But at the end of the *year*, we enjoy *all* things.

—MOLINOS

# SELF SEEKING, IN THE SEEKING OF GOD

God loves not the believer who does the most, nor who feels the most, nor who thinks the most cleverly and best, nor even that one who shows the greatest love, but He loves him who suffers the most.

I am aware that in telling you that a deeper prayer is a prayer that does not depend on outward senses nor on those things which are pleasing to our natural man, that we are speaking of something that requires the martyrdom of some parts of us. But, please remember, we are also speaking of something that pleases the Lord.

When there is no emotional experience nor intellectual insight into His way, the enemy may suggest to you that God has not spoken. But your Lord is not impressed with a multitude of words. He is impressed with the purity of the intent of your heart. He wishes to see the inward part of you humbled, quiet, and totally surrendered to Him and to His will, whatever it may be. You may not find emotions to produce such a relationship, but you will find a door by which you will enter into your nothingness and His all.

There are those people who *have* begun a practice of collecting their inmost being but turned away from it almost immediately because they did not find any *pleasure* in it! There was no sense of God, there was no power, there was no sense of being pleased with their own thought, or being impressed with the way they formed their words and sentences to God. Actually all of these approaches to God *are nothing but a hunt for sensible pleasures.* This, to God, is but self love and seeking after self. It is really not a seeking after God at all.

It is necessary that you suffer a little pain and a little dryness. Without thinking about how much time you have lost or what other losses you have sustained, come to the Lord with reverence, paying no attention to dryness and sterility. You will find eternal reward.

The more your outward man delights in some sort of pleasure in prayer, the less delight there is in the Lord. But the less you care for the outward thrills of spiritual things...ah, *here* is something which delights the Lord.

—MOLINOS

# A Commitment Established

Many have said this to me: "I've come to the Lord with perfect resignation toward all things. I have given myself to His presence by an act of faith. Yet I have not acquired any improvement. The reason is, my thoughts are so distracted that I cannot fix them upon God."

Don't be upset or discouraged; you have lost neither time nor merit. Do not lay aside your quest. When you come before the Lord, it is not necessary that you think upon the Lord. It is only necessary that you continue in your progress.

Your imagination may ramble over an infinite number of thoughts, yet, I assure you, the Lord has not left. Continue your perseverance in prayer. Remember that He prays within you, and He prays in spirit and in truth. The distraction of the mind—which is not intended—does not rob the prayer of its fruit.

But, I am asked, "Am I not at least to remember that I am in the presence of God? Am I not to say to Him, 'Lord, You abide within me and I give myself wholly to Thee'? Surely I should at least pray this."

No, there is no necessity for it. You have a desire to pray and to that end you went before Him. Faith and intention are always enough. These always continue. The simpler your remembrance is—without words or thoughts—the better foundation you lay for an undistorted relationship with the Lord who abides in you.

I am also asked, "Would it not be proper to say, 'Lord, I believe Your majesty is here'?" This is the same as the above. With the eyes of faith the spirit within you sees God, believes in Him and stands in His presence. The inmost portion of your being has no need to say, "My God, Thou art here." Believe.

Your spirit always believes.

Your spirit *knows* He is there.

Go, then, to that place where belief and knowing are always present.

And how do you go there? By faith alone.

When the time to be before the Lord has come, know that your friend *faith*, and your friend *intention*, will guide and conduct you to God. You arrive there by means of an act of faith and by a perfect resignation on your part as you wait in His presence.

—MOLINOS

## YOUR OCCUPATIONS AND YOUR CALL

Your daily occupations are not contrary to your Lord's will. Your occupation is not against the resignation to His will which you presented to Him. You see, resignation encompasses all the activities of your daily life. Whether it be study, reading, preaching, earning your living, doing business, or the like...you are resigned to whatever it is that comes into your life each day, each hour, each moment. Whatever happens in your life is, in itself, *His will*. You have not left that resignation of will *nor* have you left His presence.

If you are drawn away from Him—if you are drawn away from prayer—revert to God, return to His presence—then renew an act of faith and renew an acquiescence to His will.

And what of dryness? Dryness is good and holy, and *cannot* take you from the Divine presence. *Do not call dryness a distraction*!

When a man sets out on a journey to a great city, every step he takes is voluntary; he does not need to say, "I wish to go to the great city, I wish to go to the great city." That first step is an indication of his intention. He journeys without saying it, but he cannot journey without intending it.

—MOLINOS

# OBEDIENCE

You will never attain to the mountain of internal peace if you govern yourself according to your own will. This self nature of your soul must be conquered. Your directions, your judgment, your disposition to rebel must be subjected and reduced to ashes. How? In the fire of obedience, for it is there that you will find out if you are truly a follower of Divine love or self love. There must come a holocaust of your own values and judgments and will.

One of God's servants once said:

It would be better that you gather dung by obedience than be caught up into the third heaven by your own will.

Now, everyone enjoys the idea of honoring and obeying *superiors*. But it is also necessary, if you are to follow the inward way, to obey and honor your *inferiors* as well.

What is true obedience? Obedience, to be perfect, must be voluntary; it must be pure and cheerful. But most of all it must be *internal*. I would add that it must also be blind and persevering.

Volunteer to obey without fear; and *never* engage in obedience if there is fear. Obedience that is *pure* has no personal interest or thought of gain for oneself. Pure obedience is solely for the gain of God. Obedience is ready at any time, with no excuse and no delay. It is *cheerful*, without inward resentment, and *internal*, because it must not be external.

Obedience must proceed from the heart, *blind* because it must put aside a judgmental nature and private judgment.

—MOLINOS

# HUMILITY

There are two kinds of humility: one false and counterfeit, the other true.

False humility belongs to those who avoid esteems and who avoid all honor so that they may be taken as being humble. They go out of their way to speak often of just how very evil they are. (They do this so that they may be thought of as good.) Inside, they really do know their own misery yet they utterly despise the thought that *anyone else* would know. This is feigned humility; that is secret and hidden pride, nothing more.

There is also true humility. True humility never thinks of humility. Those who have it act with patience and live and die in God. They care not for themselves nor anything created. They suffer molestation with joy and desire nothing from it other than to walk in the footsteps of their despised Lord. They do not care to be thought of well by the world and are content with what God gives them. They are convicted of their own faults with *calm* shame!

There is no injury which can disturb them nor trouble that can vex them, no prosperity that can make them proud.

True humility is an inward thing and has nothing to do with *external acts*. (Taking the lowest place, being quiet, dressing poorly, speaking submissively, humping the shoulders, shutting the eyes, sighing effectively, speaking of your own faults, and calling yourself miserable. Do you really think such conduct is going to convince God that you are humble?) Instead, there is *simply* knowledge: an understanding of what the self nature really is! It is an internal understanding, not carried about as profound knowledge. There is no sense of believing one is humble...not even if an angel were to reveal such things.

Two things must be discovered: the greatness of God and the vastness of the devastation of the fall as pertaining to your own soul. It is an understanding so vast that no tongue can express it. From this revelation proceeds a glimpse of the grace of God...a grace which takes pleasure in encompassing that person with the pure goodness of God.

—MOLINOS

# ABANDONMENT AND SUFFERING

You must be patient in all the suffering that God sends you. If your love for the Lord is pure, you will love Him as much on Calvary as on Mt. Tabor. The Lord Jesus loved His Father on Mt. Tabor where He was transfigured, but He loved Him no less on Calvary where He was crucified. Surely, then, you should love the Lord as much on Calvary, for it was there that He made the greatest display of His love.

There is a possibility that you might make a mistake concerning your abandonment to the Lord. You may abandon yourself to the Lord hoping and expecting always to be caressed and loved and spiritually blessed by Him. You who have given yourself to the Lord during some pleasant season, please take note of this: If you gave yourself to Him to be *blessed* and to be *loved*, you cannot suddenly turn around and take back your life at another season...when you are being *crucified*!

Nor will you find any comfort from man when you have been put on the cross. Any comfort that comes to you when you are knowing the cross comes to you from the Lord.

You must learn to love the cross. He who does not love the cross does not love the things of God. (See Matthew 16:23.) It is impossible for you to truly love the Lord without loving the cross. The believer who loves the cross finds that even the bitterest things that come his way are sweet. The Scripture says, "To the hungry soul every bitter thing is sweet" (Prov. 27:7b).

How much do you desire to hunger after God? You will hunger after God, and find Him, in the same proportion that you hunger after the cross.

Here is a true spiritual principle that the Lord will not deny: God gives us the cross, and then the cross gives us God.
—GUYON

# ABANDONMENT AND A HOLY LIFE

What is the result of walking continually before God in a state of abandonment? The ultimate result is godliness. Once you have made this relationship with God part of your life, godliness is easily within your reach.

What do we mean by godliness? Godliness is something that comes from God. If you are faithful to learn this simple way to experience your Lord, you will take possession of God. And as you possess Him, you will inherit all His traits. This is godliness: The more you possess God, the more you are made like Him.[1]

But it must be a godliness that has grown from *within* you. If godliness is not from deep within you, it is only a mask. The mere outward appearance of godliness is as changeable as a garment. But when godliness is produced in you from the Life that is deep within you—then that godliness is real, lasting, and the genuine essence of the Lord. "The King's daughter is all glorious within" (Ps. 45:13a).

How, then, is godliness achieved?

The Christian who has learned to be abandoned to Jesus Christ and who walks in a life of abandonment to Him, practices godliness in the highest degree. But you would never hear such a person claim to possess any particular spirituality at all. Why? Because that Christian has become totally united with God. It is the Lord Himself who is leading that believer into this very thorough practice of godliness.

The Lord is very jealous over any saint who is utterly abandoned to Him. He does not let that believer have any pleasures at all outside of Himself.

Is abandonment the only thing necessary to bring us into godliness? No, but if you become faithful in following everything that has been said thus far, godliness *will* come. But do not forget that *suffering* is included in the experience of abandonment. It is the *fire* of suffering which will bring forth the *gold* of godliness.

—GUYON

# A NEW LOOK AT CONFESSION OF SIN

Where does *confession* of sin and *examination* of your life concerning sin fit into the life of a Christian following this path? How does he deal with these important matters? Let us take this chapter to open up a clearer, *higher* view of self-examination and of confession of sin.

It is commonly taught that self-examination is something that should always precede confession of sin. Though this may be correct, the *manner* of self-examination is dictated by the level of your Christian experience.

I would recommend for a Christian whose spiritual state has actually advanced to the stage which was described in the preceding chapters that when you come to the Lord concerning sin and confession, you do this: *Lay your entire soul open before God.* You can be certain that the Lord will not fail to enlighten you concerning your sin. Your Lord will shine as a light in you; and through His shining, He will allow you to see the nature of all your faults.

You might say that when this brilliant light, which is Christ Himself, shines on you and in you, you are under examination. An examination is being given to you by God when this happens. Since it is your Lord who is doing this, and no one else, you should simply remain peaceful and calm before Him as He carries out this exposing.

Depend upon your Lord, not on yourself, to expose your sin and to show you the extent of your sin.

Please understand this fact: It is not *your* diligence, it is not *your* examination of yourself that will enlighten you concerning your sin. Instead, it is God who does all the revealing.

You see, if you try to be the one who does the examining, there is a very good chance that you will *deceive* yourself. You will never *really* allow yourself to see your true state. That is the simple fact about the nature of your own self-love. "*We* call the evil *good*, and the good evil" (see Is. 5:20).

Ah, not so when you come to your Lord. He can be so thorough, so exacting, and so demanding! There, before Him, you are in full exposure before the Sun of Righteousness. His divine beams make even your smallest faults visible. The proper way to deal with sin becomes so evident. You must

47

abandon yourself into the hands of God, both in self-examination and in the confession of your sins.

A Christian does not begin his spiritual experience with the Lord on this level which I am describing. On the other hand, he can, through this "prayer of simplicity," eventually arrive at this level.

—GUYON

# UNDER THE DIVINE LIGHT

Once you have established such a relationship with your Lord, you will soon discover that no fault in you escapes the reproof of God. For instance, as soon as you commit a sin, you are immediately rebuked by an inward sense. It will be a kind of deep, inward burning...a tender confusion. You see, *all* things are exposed under the piercing glance of your Lord. He will not allow *any* sin to be hidden or concealed.

As for you, when the Lord has firmly established this relationship, you will have the sense that He has so completely found you out that each time His light focuses on the sin in your life, you have only one course. All you can do is turn very simply to Him and there bear all the pain and correction which He inflicts.

*Continue* in this experience with your Lord. After a period of time of experiencing Him in this way, the Lord will become more and more the *constant* examiner of your soul. It will not be *you* examining yourself, nor will it be seasonal. It will be the Lord, *constantly*.

If you remain faithful in giving yourself up to the Lord in this way, you will come to realize that the divine light of your Lord can really reveal your heart far more effectively than *all* your efforts ever could.

—GUYON

# DISTRACTIONS

Now that we have explored some of the encounters you will have in this venture—some of the things the Lord will introduce to you and some of the things He will demand from you—let us set this chapter aside for a practical matter. As you have read in previous chapters, there will be distractions, especially at the outset. And for quite some time afterward, your mind will be distracted from prayer. Let us take a brief look at this problem.

How do you deal with those things that distract; how do you handle those things that draw you away from the inmost part of your being? If you should sin (or even if it is only a matter of being distracted by some circumstances around you), what should you do?

*You must instantly turn within to your spirit.*

Once you have departed from God, you must return to Him as quickly as possible. There, once more with Him, receive any penalty He chooses to inflict.

But here is one thing you must be very careful about: Do *not* become distressed because your mind has wandered away. Always guard yourself from being anxious because of your faults. First of all, such distress only stirs up the soul and distracts you to outward things. Secondly, your distress really springs from a secret root of pride. What you are experiencing is, in fact, a love of your own worth.

To put it in other words, you are simply hurt and upset at seeing what you *really* are.

If the Lord should be so merciful as to give you a true spirit of His humility, you will not be surprised at your faults, your failures, or even your own basic nature.

The more clearly you see your true self, the clearer you also see how miserable your self-nature really is; and the more you will abandon your whole being to God. Seeing that you have such a desperate need of Him, you will press toward a more intimate relationship with Him.

This is the way you should walk, just as the Lord Himself has said: "I will instruct you and teach you in the way you shall go. I will guide you with My eyes" (see Ps. 32:8).

—GUYON

# DANGERS OF TEMPTATION

Temptations, as well as distractions, are a major problem you will encounter at the outset of your adventure into God. Be very careful in your attitude toward them. If you attempt to struggle directly with these temptations, you will only strengthen them; and in the process of this struggle, your soul will be drawn away from its intimate relationship with the Lord.

You see, a close, intimate relationship to Christ should always be your soul's only purpose. Therefore, when you are tempted toward sin or toward outward distractions—no matter the time, no matter the place, nor the provocation—*simply turn away* from that sin.

And as you turn, draw nearer to your Lord.

It is that simple.

What does a little child do when he sees something that frightens him or confuses him? He doesn't stand there and try to fight the thing. He will, in fact, hardly look at the thing that frightens him. Rather, the child will quickly run into the arms of his mother.

There, in those arms, he is safe.

In exactly the same way, you should turn from the dangers of temptation and *run* to your God!

*God is in the midst of her, she shall not be moved: God shall help her, and that right early* (Psalm 46:5).

You and I are very weak. At our best we are *very* weak. If you, in your weakness, attempt to attack your enemies, you will often find yourself wounded. Just as frequently, you will even find yourself defeated.

—GUYON

# THE CONSTANT STATE

We will begin this chapter with this simple point: Your spiritual experiences fall into two categories—those that are external (surface) and those that take place internally, deep within your being. There are activities or actions that you form: some are surface; some are deeper.

Your external activities are those which can be seen outwardly. They have to do with, more or less, physical things. Now this you must see: There is no real goodness in them, no spiritual growth in them, and very *little* experience of Christ!

Of course, there is an exception: If your outward actions are a result (a by-product) of something that has taken place deep within you, then these outward actions *do* receive spiritual value and they *do* possess real goodness. But outward activities have only as much spiritual value as they receive from their source.

Our way, therefore, is clear. We must give our full attention to those activities that take place deep within our inmost being. *These* are the activities of the Spirit. The Spirit is inward, not outward. You turn inward to your spirit and, in so doing, turn away from outward activities and outward distractions.

Inward activity begins by simply turning within to Jesus Christ, for that is where He is, within your spirit.

You should continually be turning within to God.

Give Him all your attention; pour out all the strength of your being purely on Him.

Reunite all the motions of your heart in the holiness of God. (Apocrypha)

David expressed it so well when he said, "I will keep my whole strength for You." (See Psalm 59:9.)

How is this done? By earnestly turning to God, who is always there within you.

Isaiah said, "Return to your heart." (See Isaiah 46:8.) Each of us, by sinning, has turned from our heart, and it is only the heart that God desires.

*My son, give me your heart and let your eyes delight in my ways* (see Proverbs 23:26).

What does it mean to give your whole heart to God? To give your whole heart to God is to have all the energy of your soul always centered on Him.

It is in this way we are conformed to His will.

If you are new in this voyage, your spirit is not yet strong. Your soul is easily turned to outward, physical things; it is very easy for you to become distracted from the Lord, your Center.

How far you turn away from Him will depend on how much you yield to the distractions and how far you allow yourself to be drawn away to surface things. In like manner, the means you use to return to God will depend on how far you have turned from Him. If you have only turned slightly, only the slightest turning again will be necessary.

As soon as you notice yourself straying from the Lord, you should *deliberately* turn your attention within to the living God. Re-enter your spirit; return at once to that place where you really belong: in Him. The more complete that turning is, the more complete will be your return to the Lord.

Rest assured that you will remain there—in God—just as long as your attention is centered upon the Lord Jesus Christ. What will hold you there? You will be held there by the powerful influence of that simple, unpretentious turning of your heart to God.

Repeat this simple turning within to the Lord again and again, as often as you are distracted. Be assured that eventually this turning will become your consistent experience.

—GUYON

# TURNING WITHIN

What do I mean by this continuous inner abiding?

To be *continuously* turned deep inside simply means that, having turned within to God—by a direct act—you have remained in His presence. You have no further need to keep turning to Christ; you already abide with Him in the chambers of your spirit. The only time you need to make a point of turning again is when your abiding is interrupted for some reason.

At this point in your spiritual life, you should not concern yourself with *trying* to turn to the Lord by any outward means. You will even find it difficult to make a deliberate, outward act of turning when you have begun this inner abiding.

You see, you are already turned within to the Lord; any outward activity will only draw you away from your union with Him.

To form the act of turning within, *that* is the goal! When this act has been formed in you, it will express itself as a continual abiding in your spirit and a continuous exchange of love between you and the Lord. Once this goal is attained, there is no longer any need to seek after it by *outward* acts. You may forget the outward act of trying to love the Lord and to be loved by Him. Instead, just continue on as you are. You should simply remain near to God *by* this continuous inner abiding.

In this state of continually being turned to God, you are abiding in the love of God, and the man who abides in love abides in God. (See First John 4:16.) You rest. But what does that mean? You *rest* in the *continuously* inward act of abiding.

Now, in this state of rest, is your soul active or passive? It is active! You are not in a passive state, even if you are resting.

But what activity could there be in resting? You are resting in the act of abiding in His love. Can that be activity? Yes! Inside your spirit there is an act going on. It is a *sweet sinking into Deity.*

The inward attraction—the magnetic pull—becomes more and more powerful. Your soul, dwelling in love, is drawn by this powerful attraction and sinks continually deeper into that love.

So you see, this inward activity has become far greater than it was when your soul first began to turn inward. Under the powerful attraction of God drawing you into Himself, the inward activity has increased!

—GUYON

# GAINING THE HEART

As we draw near the close of this little book, I would like to address a word of exhortation to those Christian workers who are in charge of new converts.

Let us consider the present situation. All around us, Christians are seeking to convert the lost to Jesus Christ. What is the best way to do this? And once men have been converted, what is the best way to aid them in attaining full perfection in Christ?

The way to reach the lost is to reach them by the *heart*. If a new convert were introduced to *real prayer* and to a *true inward experience of Christ* as soon as he became converted, you would see countless numbers of converts go on to become true disciples.

On the other hand, you can see that the present way of dealing only with external matters in the life of the new convert brings little fruit. Burdening the new Christian with countless rules and all sorts of standards does not help him grow in Christ. Here is what should be done: The new Christian should be led to God.

How!

By learning to turn within to Jesus Christ *and* by giving the Lord his whole heart. If you are one of those in charge of new believers, lead them to a *real inner knowledge* of Jesus Christ. Oh, what a difference there would be in the lives of those new Christians!

Consider the results!

We would see the simple farmer, as he plowed his field, spend his days in the blessing of the presence of God. The shepherd, while watching his flocks, would have the same abandoned love for the Lord which marked the early Christians. The factory worker, while laboring with his outward man, would be renewed with strength in his inner man.

You would see each of these people put away every kind of sin from his life; all would become spiritual men and women with hearts set on knowing and experiencing Jesus Christ.

For a new Christian—for all of us in fact—the heart is all important if we are to go forward in Christ. Once the heart has been gained by God, everything else will eventually take care of itself. This is why He requires the heart above all else.

Dear reader, it is by the Lord gaining your heart, and no other way, that all your sins can be put away. If the heart could be gained, Jesus Christ would reign in peace, and the whole church would be renewed.

—GUYON

# The Ultimate Christian Attainment

We come now to the ultimate state of Christian experience. Divine Union.

This cannot be brought about merely by your own experience. Meditation will not bring divine union; neither will love, nor worship, nor your devotion, nor your sacrifice. Nor does it matter how much light the Lord gives you.

Eventually it will take an *act of God* to make union a reality.

In the Old Testament the Scripture says, "No man shall see God and live" (see Ex. 33:20). If your prayer still contains your own life, that prayer cannot see God. *Your* life will *not* know the experience of union with *His* life.

All that is of your doing, *all* that comes from your life—even your most exalted prayer—must first be destroyed before union can come about.

All the prayers that proceed from your mind are merely *preparations* for bringing you to a passive state; any and all active contemplation on your part is also just preparation for bringing you to a passive state. They are preparations. *They are not the end.* They are a *way* to the end.

The *end* is union with God!

—GUYON

# LOSS OF SELF

There is something in this universe which is the very opposite of God; it is the self. The activity of the self is the source of all the evil nature as well as all the evil deeds of man. On the other hand, the *loss* of the selfhood in the soul increases the purity of the soul! In fact, the soul's purity is increased in exact proportion to the loss of self!

As long as you employ your self-nature in any way, some faults will also continue to exist in you. But after you depart from your selfhood, no faults can exist, and all is purity and innocence.

It was the entrance of the *self*, which came into the soul as a result of the fall, that established a difference between the soul and God.

How can two things so opposite as the soul and God ever be united? How can the purity of God and the impurity of man be made one? How can the simplicity (or singleness) of God and the multiplicity (endless fickleness) of man ever melt into one element?

Certainly much more is required than just the efforts that *you* can make.

What, then, is necessary for union to be achieved? A move on the part of Almighty God Himself. This alone can ever accomplish union.

For two things to become one, the two must have similar natures. For instance, the impurity of dirt cannot be united with the purity of gold. Fire has to be introduced to destroy the dross and leave the gold pure. This is why God sends a fire to the earth (it is called His Wisdom) to destroy all that is impure in you. Nothing can resist the power of that fire. It consumes *everything*. His Wisdom burns away all the impurities in a man for one purpose: *to leave him fit for divine union.*

—GUYON

## PURIFYING THE SOUL

God wishes to make your soul pure. He purifies it by His Wisdom just as a refiner purifies metal in the furnace. *Fire is the only thing which can purify gold.*

Again, the fire that consumes us—utterly—is His highest wisdom.

This fire gradually consumes all that is earthly; it takes out all foreign matter and separates these things from the gold.

The fire seems to know that the earthly mixture cannot be changed into gold. The fire must melt and dissolve this dross by force so that it can rid the gold of every alien particle. Over and over again, the gold must be cast into the furnace until it has lost every trace of pollution. Oh, how many times the gold is plunged back into the fire—far, far more times than seem necessary. Yet you can be sure the Forger sees impurities no one else can see. The gold must return to the fire again and again until positive proof has been established that it can be no further purified.

There comes a time, at last, when the goldsmith can find no more mixture that adulterates the gold. When the fire has perfected *purity*—or should I say *simplicity*—the fire no longer touches it. If the gold remained in the furnace for an eon, its spotlessness would not be improved upon nor its substance diminished!

Now the gold is fit for the most exquisite workmanship. In the future, if the gold should get dirty and seem to lose its beauty, it is nothing more than an accidental impurity which touches only the surface. This dirt is of no hindrance to the use of the gold vessel. This foreign particle which attaches itself to the surface is a far cry from having corruption deep within the hidden nature of the gold.

Rare would be the man who would reject a pure, golden vessel because it had some external dirt on it, preferring some cheap metal only because its surface had been polished.

Please do not misunderstand me. I am not excusing sin in the life of a person in union with God. Such an idea never occurred to me. I am referring here only to natural defects; defects which God deliberately leaves even in His greatest saints, to keep them from pride and to keep them from the praise of men who judge only from outward appearance.

God allows defects to remain in the dearest of His saints so He can preserve that saint from corruption and "hide him in the secret of His presence" (see Ps. 31:20).

—GUYON

## Endnote

1. Transformation.

# DRAWING INWARD

# Let Go of Anxiety

Let your anxiety flow away like a stream. What evidence you concoct for the most imaginary situations! God permits you, despite your excellent sense, to be blind to what is right in front of you. You think you see clearly what does not exist at all. God will be glorified in your life if you yield to Him. Never make important decisions in a state of distress. You just are not able to see clearly.

When you are calm and collected, you will find the will of God more clearly known. Turn toward devotion and simplicity. Listen to God and be deaf to yourself. When you are in a place of calm and quiet rest, do all that you sense within your spirit. But to suppose you are levelheaded when you are in the agony of distress is to set yourself up to make a mistake. Any experienced spiritual counselor will tell you not to make decisions until you regain your peace and re-enter inward prayer. Never trust yourself when you are suffering greatly because your nature is so unreasonable and upset.

You say that I am trying to prevent you from doing what you should. God forbid! I do not want to encourage you or stop you. I only want you to please God. It is as clear as day that you will fail to do what God wants if you act when your old nature is feeling deeply wounded to the point of despair.

Would you do something only to make yourself happy even if it went against God's will? God forbid. Wait until you are not feeling so hurt. Be open to every alternative that God might suggest. Sacrifice anything for His sake.

—FENELON

# QUIET LEADING

I know that God will keep you. Although you do not enjoy spiritual discipline, be faithful to seeking God as much as your health will permit. I realize that eating, both physically and spiritually, does not appeal to you now. Still, you must eat to survive.

It would be good for you if you could have a few minutes of fellowship with those members of your family that you can confide in. As to whom you should talk with—be guided by your inner sense of what is right in each moment. God does not lead you with extreme emotion, and for this I am glad. Remain faithful to the still, small voice. Strong emotions and deep feelings, or seeking after signs, can be more dangerous than helpful. Your imagination is sure to run away with you. God will lead you, almost without your knowing it, if you will be faithful to come before Him quietly. Eat of Him and His word. Love Him and I will tell you to do no more. For if you love Him, everything else will work out. I am not asking you for a tender and emotional love, but simply that you lean toward love. Put God before yourself and the world and even your evil desires will begin to be transformed.

—FENELON

# CULTIVATING SILENCE

Simply bringing yourself quietly before God will do more than worrying or being too religious. Silence is so important. Even when you cannot find total silence, you might try letting others take the lead in conversations. There is no better way to quench the natural strength of your old nature than by silencing it. Guard your tongue. As you become more aware of the presence of God within, you will see how He is able to keep your words, thoughts, and desires in check. This work all happens gradually, so be patient with yourself as well as with others.

Try to practice silence as much as general courtesy permits. Silence encourages God's presence, prevents harsh words, and causes you to be less likely to say something you will regret. Silence also helps you put space between you and the world. Out of the silence that you cultivate, you will find strength to meet your needs.

No matter how much you cultivate silence, there will still be many disrupting situations in which you will find yourself against your will. God knows that you want to have much time to pray, but He still allows you to be surrounded by things that seem to prevent prayer.

Learn to love God's will more than the sweetness of self-chosen prayer. You know very well that you do not need to pray in your closet to love God. When He gives you time, take it to pray. When there is not time, be satisfied anyway. Lift up your spirit to Him without making any outward sign. Talk only when necessary. Bear the hardest things that cross your life. You need to deny yourself more than you need more light.

Be faithful in keeping silent, and God will keep you from evil when you talk.

Accept what God chooses for you. This is more important than what you choose for yourself, for you are much too easy on yourself. Day by day give yourself to God. He carries you in His arms like a mother carries her child. Believe, hope, and love like a child. Look with love and trust to your heavenly Father.

—FENELON

## COME OUT OF YOURSELF

As long as you live by your old nature you will be open to all of the injustices of men. Your temper will get you into fights, your passions will clash with your neighbors, your desires will be like tender spots open to your enemies' arrows. Everything will be against you—attacking you from all sides. If you live at the mercy of a crowd of greedy and hungry desires, then you will never find peace. You will never be satisfied because everything will bother you. You will be like an invalid who has been bedridden for many years—anywhere you are touched you will feel pain. Your self-love is terribly touchy. No matter how slightly it is insulted, it screams, "Murderer." Add to this all the insensitivity of others, their disgust at your weakness (and your disgust at theirs), and you have the children of Adam forever tormenting each other.

The only hope is to come out of yourself. Lose all your self-interest. Only then can you enjoy the true peace reserved for "men of good will." Such people have no other will but

God's. If you come to such a place, then what can harm you? You will no longer be attacked through your hopes or fears. You may be worried, inconvenienced, or distressed, but you can rest in Him. Love the hand that disciplines you. Find peace in all things—even in going to the cross. Be happy with what you have. Wish for nothing more. Surrender to God and find true peace.

—FENELON

# Live Day by Day

Your spiritual walk is a little too restless and uneasy. Simply trust God. If you come to Him, He will give you all that you need to serve Him. You really need to believe that God keeps His word. The more you trust Him, the more He will be able to give you. If you were lost in an uncrossable desert, bread would fall from heaven for you alone.

Fear nothing but to fail God. And do not even fear that so much that you let it upset you. Learn to live with your failures, and bear with the failures of your neighbors. Do you know what would be best for you? Stop trying to appear so mentally and spiritually perfect to God and man. There is a lot of refined selfishness and complacency in not allowing your faults to be revealed. Be simple with God. He loves to communicate Himself to simple people. Live day by day, not in your own strength, but by completely surrendering to God.

—FENELON

# INNER CALM

I hear you are having problems sleeping. You must wait for sleep in peace. If you let your imagination run away with you when you are trying to sleep, you may never get to sleep. I will not think that you are growing spiritually until I see that you have become calm enough to sleep peacefully without restlessness.

Ask God for calmness and inner rest. I know what you are thinking—that controlling your imagination does not depend on yourself. Excuse me, please, but it depends very much on yourself! When you cut off all the restless and unprofitable thoughts that you can control, you will greatly reduce all those thoughts which are involuntary. God will guard your imagination if you do your part in not encouraging your wayward thoughts.

Live in peace. Your imagination is too active; it will eat you up! Your inward life will die of starvation. All that buzzing in your mind is like bees in a beehive. If you excite your thoughts, they will grow angry and sting you! How can you expect God to speak in His gentle and inward voice when you make so much noise? Be quiet and you will hear God speak. Live in the peace of Jesus.

—FENELON

# MISUNDERSTANDING PRAYER

Return to prayer and inward fellowship with God no matter what the cost. You have withered your spirit by chasing this wish of yours without knowing if God wanted this for you.

Don't spend your time making plans that are just cobwebs—
a breath of wind will come and blow them away. You have
withdrawn from God and now you find that God has withdrawn the sense of His presence from you. Return to Him and
give Him everything without reservation. There will be no
peace for you otherwise. Let go of all your plans—God will do
what He sees best for you.

Even if you were able to accomplish your plans through
earthly means, God would not bless them. Offer Him your
tangled mess and He will turn everything toward His own
merciful purpose. You must learn to let go of everything
whether God ever gives you what you so eagerly desire or not.
The most important thing is to go back to communion with
God—even if it seems dry and you are easily distracted.

—FENELON

# INNER REALITIES

Avoid anything that drains or excites you. Your prayer
life will dry up if you don't. Don't expect to feed your inward
life if you live only for what is outward. You really must learn
to renounce all that makes you too outspoken in your conversation. How are you going to cultivate an inner silence if you
are always talking? You cannot want God and the things of the
world at the same time. Don't you realize that your prayer will
be affected by what you cultivate in your daily life?

Fear your excessive enthusiasm, your taste for things of
the world, and your hidden ambitions. Don't get so excited
over politics and parties. If you get too worked up, it will be

harder to calm yourself before God. Speak little and work steadily. Let actions take the place of your flowery words.

After you learn to deal with your wandering thoughts, you must learn to come to God to renew your strength. Learn to do this even amidst the mundane tasks of the day. Keep looking to the Lord for His gentle leading. But don't be so noisy that you can't hear Him!

You will lose your way the minute you decide to go your own way. When you seek God's will alone, you find it everywhere, and you cannot go astray. Wanting what God wants always puts you on a straight path. The future is not yet yours; it may never be. Live in the present moment. Tomorrow's grace is not given to you today. The present moment is the only place where you can touch the eternal realm.

—FENELON

# REAL PRAYER

Real prayer is nothing more than loving God. Prayer is not made great by a lot of words, for God knows your inmost feelings before you say them. True prayer comes from the spirit. You pray only for what you really desire. If you do not see what you are desiring from the depths of your heart, your prayer is deceitful. You could pass whole days "praying," but if you do not pray from your deepest, inmost desires, you are not praying.

You pray without ceasing when there is true love in your heart, and when there is a desire born of God there. Love, hidden in the depths of the spirit, prays constantly even when your mind needs to attend to something else. Love asks God to give you what you need and to regard your sincerity above your human weakness.

God's love within you removes even the slightest faults and purifies you like a consuming fire. The Spirit within you asks for all things according to the will of God. Even when you are busy with outward things there is still a constantly burning fire within you. This fire, which cannot be put out, encourages a secret prayer which is like a lamp always burning before the throne of God. "I sleep but my heart is awake."

There are two things that will help you keep this spirit of prayer: regular time set aside to be with God, and coming back to God as much as you can during the day. Stay away from people who distract you too much or who excite your passions!

The first fruit of a sincere love for God is the earnest desire to do all that you can to please your Beloved. To do any less is to love yourself before God. God forbid! Cost what it may, you must be willing to do all that He asks without reservation.

Do what you should before you go out to enjoy yourself. People who neglect their duties to "spend more time with God" deceive themselves. You won't get closer to God by being irresponsible and calling it "spiritual." Real union with God is to do all that is required of you by God, no matter what you feel.

Make sure you make time for God. Those who are in important positions are often busy and will be tempted to leave time for communion with God until last. Guess what? You will never have any time for God. Be firm with yourself. Don't let the confusion of the day crowd out your time with

God. This may sound too strict, but you will soon fall apart if you don't listen to what I have to say about this.

—FENELON

# INWARD SILENCE

God is your true friend and will always give you the counsel and comfort you need. Do not resist Him! Learn to listen to Him in silence so that you won't miss a word of what He says to you. You know a lot about outward silence, but little about inward silence. You must practice quieting your restless imagination. Stop listening to your unrenewed mind and the kind of logic it has! Get used to coming to God and asking Him for help when He asks you for something you are afraid to give.

Your sensitivity to the smallest affairs shows how much you need God to tear the things of the world from you. You are making great progress when you begin to give God all the childish attitudes you have, and let him deal with the "small" problems of your life. You need not make a deep show of spirituality—just let God work on your everyday issues. You can die to yourself in the course of your everyday life—you don't need to go out into the desert, or on some high mountain to be spiritual. All God asks of you is to give Him what He directs you to. To do this you must watch and pray. Cultivate trust in God—not your vanity or curiosity or lazy nature.

—FENELON

# PRAYER OF SURRENDER

My God, I want to give myself to you. Give me the courage to do this. My spirit within me sighs after you. Strengthen my will. Take me. If I don't have the strength to give You everything, then draw me by the sweetness of Your love. Lord, who do I belong to, if not to You? What a horror to belong to myself and to my passions! Help me to find all my happiness in You, for there is no happiness outside of You.

Why am I afraid to break out of my chains? Do the things of this world mean more to me than You? Am I afraid to give myself to You? What a mistake! It is not even I who would give myself to You, but You who would give Yourself to me. Take my heart.

What joy it is to be with You, to be quiet so that I might hear Your voice! Feed me and teach me out of Your depths. Oh God, You only make me love You. Why should I fear to give You everything and draw close to You? To be left to the world is more frightening than this! Your mercy can overcome any obstacle. I am unworthy of You, but I can become a miracle of Your grace.

—FENELON

# Two Kinds of Prayer

What is prayer? It is an ascent of the mind to God. He is above us all, and we cannot see Him, therefore we converse with Him. Such prayer as this is the simplest form of prayer. But this is a kind of prayer that is essentially only a mental discourse with God.

But when the believer fixes his attention on the face of his Lord without requiring consideration, reasoning, without need of proofs to be convinced of anything, *this* is a higher prayer.

There is a view of your Lord in which reason, meditation and thought do not play a large part. In the first kind of prayer, one *thinks* upon God; in the other, one *beholds* Him. The second is a purer practice.

Once a ship has arrived in the harbor, the voyage is over, is it not? In the same way, for us to truly lay hold of God there may be some means used to arrive there. But once those means have been established, and once the end has been laid hold of, you lay aside the means. That is, you lay down the method.

Sometimes a good place to begin *is* with rational prayer. Nonetheless, rational prayer is but a method to bring you to a deeper, more tranquil relationship with your Lord. When you have arrived at this second level of prayer you put an end to all rational discussion; instead, you rest. A simple vision of God, seeing Him and loving Him (and very gently rejecting all the images which come into your mind): *This* is more meaningful prayer.

The mind is calm in the Divine presence. Everything within you is collected, *centered* and fixed wholly on Him.

It behooves you, you who would seek a deeper walk with your Lord, to soon lay aside clearly defined intelligibles. In short, lay aside *everything* and cast yourself into the bosom of a loving God. Eventually this Lord of yours will restore to you all you have dropped, while at the same time increasing you in strength and power. (I speak of a power to *love* Him more ardently.) In turn this love will maintain you in *all* circumstances that may come into your life. Be sure that the love which you pour out toward Him (which love He Himself will give you) is worth more than all the actions which you can ever perform. There is little you can do for God; there is so very little in this lifetime you will ever really come to understand of Him, I care not how wise you are, nor how much you study. But, oh! You can love Him a great deal.

—MOLINOS

# THE DESIRE TO LAY ASIDE OUTWARD PRAYER

I would like to point out some matters which you might expect to encounter on a journey toward a deeper relationship with your Lord. Eventually you may come to a place where you find yourself unable to go on with an intelligent prayer life, *or*, at least, you will begin to *desire* to lay aside such prayer. This will not come to you by way of your natural inclinations nor because you are in a period of dryness, but rather it is provoked by the Lord Himself, deep within you. This inclination to lay aside a more outward prayer is the natural end of seeking, and hungering, for something deeper.

Another possibility you may notice is that the reading of books becomes a tedious matter. Perhaps this is because they do not deal with inward matters.

Another experience you might encounter is a growing knowledge of your own *self*-nature, an abhorring of your sins, and an insight into the deeper nature of God, and His holiness.

What you are longing for is something that only the Lord can give you.

You will not fully know the inward life that I speak of until you know what it means for your own will to be conformed to that of the Divine will. If you, the believer, would have everything succeed, if you would have everything come to pass according to your own will, then you will never know the way of peace. Such a person will also lead a bitter and empty life, always restless and disturbed, never touching the way of peace. This deeper walk is in total conformity to the will of God.

—MOLINOS

# EXPECT FAILURE

You should know that every Christian who is called by the Lord to the inward way is, nonetheless, a Christian who is full of confusion and doubt, and one who has failed (and will fail) in this deeper level of prayer. In fact, you may get the impression that the Lord no longer helps you in prayer as He once did. You may feel you are losing a great deal of time and making no progress. Confusion and perplexity are bound to follow. Nonetheless, do not stop, and do not let anyone, even someone who is older in the faith, keep you from pursuing a deeper relationship with your Lord.

What is really happening in your life? Are you *really* experiencing failure? Not at all.

The Lord is calling you to walk by *faith* in His Divine presence. With a simple vision of your Lord and with intense love toward Him—like a little child would have toward its mother—cast yourself into the gentle bosom of your Lord. The spirit should become like a little child, and a *beggar*, in the presence of God.

Such a relationship to your Lord—especially in times of *perceived* failure—is *easy*. It is also *the most secure* relationship you can enter into with Him. The level of prayer you are seeking is a prayer free from a wandering imagination and from reasoning. Both of these are so distracting, and can get you involved in speculation and introspection...especially during periods of failure!

—MOLINOS

# THE LIMITATION OF OUTWARD PRAYER

Throughout the ages it has been the common view of spiritual believers that the believer cannot attain to a deeper walk in relationship to his Lord by means of prayer that is mostly consideration, requests, meditation, reasoning and a great deal of objective discussion. At best such prayer is only of benefit at the *outset* of the spiritual quest.

Further, it has been observed, such surface and objective prayer is something that is learned very quickly.

But the relationship to Christ we are discussing here is *not* learned quickly.

If you continue on in typical—outward—prayer (prayer that is most common to those who pray), and if such practice continues year after year without a great deal of upward progression, then you are wasting a great deal of time. Why seek the Lord by means of straining the brain, in searching for some place to go to pray, in selecting points to discuss, and in straining to find a God without...when you have Him within you?

St. Augustine summed it up so beautifully:

Lord, I went wandering like a stray sheep, seeking you with anxious reasoning weighted within me. I wearied myself much in looking for you without. Yet you had your habitation within me. If only I had desired you, and panted after you. I went around the streets and squares of the cities of this world and I found you not, because in vain I sought without for you who were within.

We simply shall not find our God without. Nor shall we find Him by means of reasoning and logic and surface information. Each of us has Him present within us. There seems to be a blindness in those believers who always seek God, cry for Him, long for Him, invoke His name, pray to Him daily, while never discovering that they themselves are a living Temple and His one *true* habitation.

Their own spirit is the seat and throne of a God who continually rests within them.

Who, then, but a fool would look for an instrument of God without when he knew that it was within his own door? Or who will ever be filled when he is hungry and yet refuses to ever taste? Yet, this is the life lived by many good men, always seeking, never enjoying. Their works are imperfect.

Nor should you think the spiritual way is difficult...nor is it only for those high minds.

Your Lord made it clear this was not true when He chose His apostles. They were ignorant and lowly. He spoke to the Father saying, "I thank you Father, that you have hid these things from the wise; You revealed them to babes." It is so clear that we are not going to attain to those deep things, nor those deep places within us, by reasoning or by surface prayer.

—MOLINOS

## Two Spiritual Experiences

In all your journey as a believer, you will have two categories of spiritual experiences. One is tender, delightful, and loving. The other can be quite obscure, dry, dark and desolate. God gives us this first one to gain us; He gives us the second to purify us.

First He deals with you as if you were only a child. *Then* He begins to deal with you as though you were a strong man. In the first there is a great deal of your Christian experience tied to that which you can sense outwardly. (You are attracted by these nice pleasant and outward experiences; in fact you can even become addicted to them.) But the other category of Christian experience calls for a believer to no longer mind the outward senses. Rather he must know warfare against his own passions, and attain to a will that is in complete agreement and concert with the Lord...this is the proper occupation of us all.

Dry spells are the instrument of God, for *your* good. Yes, it is true in such times, your five senses have been deprived and all *outward* progress of *outward* piety ends. Know this: In such times you are either going to leave off prayer, and perhaps even a large part of your Christian walk, *or* you will be driven to a comfort which has nothing to do with the outward senses.

There is always a veil that comes to us in relationship to times of dryness; it is a time when we do not know what He is doing. If we always knew what His working was (as He works *on* our outward man and works *in* our inward man) we would become very presumptuous. We would imagine we were doing quite well if we always knew what He was doing, would we not? We might even reckon that we had drawn very near to God. Such a conclusion would soon be our undoing.

A dependence upon outward circumstances, everything about your spiritual understanding depending on your outward senses—*all* of this must go by the way. How? By dryness!

The Lord uses these arid lands, these desert places.

The farmer sows in one season, and he reaps in another; God is quite like this. It is *in His time* that He gives you strength against temptation. (Often that strength comes at a time you least think it might.)

What are the fruits of a believer who persists in seeking the Lord in a deeper way in such times of dryness? Should you survive such periods and humbly persevere after Him, what might you expect to be the result of dry spells?

You will learn the gift of perseverance, which has many fruits and advantages. You will develop a weariness toward the things of this world little by little, and by slow degrees, the desires of your past life lose their strength; new ones toward your Lord arise.

You will also learn a reflection and concentration on things in which you formerly had virtually no interest.

When you are on the verge of committing some evil, you will sense some warning deep within you, a warning that will restrain you from the execution of that evil. Your attachment to that earthly pleasure will be cut, or you will flee from that situation or from that conversation, or whatever it is, that is drawing you away. You will be putting aside things in your life which never previously disturbed your conscience.

—MOLINOS

# Persevering in Prayer

When you do fall into some fault, trusting it will be some light one, you will find a reproof within you which will afflict you greatly.

There will gradually grow in you a willingness, perhaps even a sense within you, that you are now willing to suffer and do the will of God.

There will also gradually grow up in you an inclination toward things holy (perhaps even an ease in dealing with the self-nature, and with passions, and even with the enemy that waits in the way).

You will learn to know your self-nature and despise it. Without this deep insight—even this revelation—all other attempts at "spirituality" are invalid. You will experience a great esteem for God, an esteem that is far above all other creatures. You will have a firm resolution not to allow yourself to abandon His presence, because leaving Him, abandoning Him, would be in itself the greater suffering and the greater loss.

You will have a sense of peace within you. A confidence in God's sovereignty and even a detachment from all other things.

*All* this can come about as a result of your persevering in prayer that is *dry* and *arid*. You will not feel these things when you are in prayer, but later, perhaps *much* later—*in His time*—when He and He alone considers it the appropriate time for you—these attributes will begin to appear.

All of the things that I have just mentioned, plus much more, are like new buds that arise from this little tree of spiritual prayer. Would you abandon such a small bush just because it seems to be dry, and because there is not much fruit on it, or because its buds seem so small and because it *appears* that there will never be any reaping? Dear one, be constant, persevere. Your soul will profit thereby.

—MOLINOS

# TRANQUILLITY

Remember that it is *tranquillity* which you will use to repel wandering thoughts and temptations.

When you go to prayer, deliver your entire being into the hands of God, and do so with perfect resignation and with an act of faith; believe that you stand in His presence and remain there quietly. And, as I have said, with tranquillity.

(Do you fret over a wandering mind? Is this evidence of a life totally given over into His hands, accepting all things from His hands?)

Let me illustrate. If you have given a precious jewel to a dear friend, once it has been given to him, it is not necessary for you to repeat, "I give you this jewel, I give you this jewel." All that needs to be done is to let him keep it! Do not take it from him! Surely, if you do not take it back from him, it is certain that you have given it to him.

Do not labor in constantly reminding the Lord of your commitment and resignation to Him. You have given Him the jewel; do not take it back.

And how would you take it back?

Only by committing some noteworthy fault against His Divine will.

The mere business of getting ready to go before the Lord is great preparation. It awakens your lively sense toward what it is you are doing.

Hold always before you this simple fact, that your response in God abides in peace.

—MOLINOS

# Two Kinds of Spiritual Men

There are two kinds of spiritual men. And they are contrary to one another.

83

Some tell us that the mysteries and the sufferings of Christ are always to be meditated upon. Others, at the other extreme, tell us that the only true prayer is an internal thing, offered up in quiet and silence, a *centering* upon the exaltation and supreme Deity of God.

Let us look at our Lord. He has said, "I AM the Way, the Truth, and the LIFE." Before anyone can come into the presence of Divinity, he must be washed with the precious blood of the Redeemer...hence we are certain we should *not* lay aside the redemption of our Lord. But neither should we tell a believer who has learned something of living within his spirit that he should always be reasoning, meditating and considering the suffering and death of our Lord.

As long as an outward prayer nourishes and benefits, a believer should follow outward prayer. It is only when a longing for something more is sensed in the heart that the pilgrimage into the inward way should be considered. It is up to the Lord alone to take us from one to the other. St. Paul, in writing to the Colossians, exhorted them as well as us that whatever we do, whether it is in word or deed, we should do it in the name and for the sake of Jesus Christ. May God grant that you and I, in Him and through Him alone, may arrive at that state which most pleases him.

—MOLINOS

# THREE KINDS OF SILENCE

There are three kinds of silence: a silence of words, a silence of desires, and a silence of thoughts.

The first is perfect. The second is even more perfect and the third is the most perfect.

In the first, the silence of words, there is virtue that is acquired. In the second, the silence of desires, quietness is obtained; and in the third, the silence of thoughts...*this* is the goal: the internal recollection of all of your senses. To lay hold of the silence of thought is to arrive and abide at the center of your being, where Christ dwells.

By not speaking, desiring, nor reasoning, we reach the central place of the inward walk—that place where God speaks to our inward man. It is there that God communicates Himself to our spirit; and there, in the inmost depths of our being, He teaches us Himself. He guides us to this place where He alone speaks His most secret and hidden heart. You must enter into this through all silence if you would hear the Divine Voice within you.

Forsaking the world will not accomplish this. Nor renouncing your desires. No, not even if you should renounce all things created!

What then?

Rest is found only in this threefold silence...only before an open door, where God may communicate Himself to you. It is in that place that He transforms you into Himself.

—MOLINOS

# Internal and External Spirituality

There are two kinds of spiritual people, those who are internally spiritual and those who are externally spiritual.

Those who are spiritual externally seek God by reasoning, by the things they imagine, by long periods of consideration in which they go down many avenues of thought.

These people endure pain to obtain virtue. They delight in talking about God. They delight in being very fervent in love, and even in being skilled in prayer. They are seeking to obtain greatness by doing things. They believe that God abides close to them only by their *doing* the above-mentioned things.

What is this?

This is the way of beginners! Experience has shown that many believers, even after 50 years of this external exercise, are void of God. They are also full of themselves, having nothing of the true spiritual man except the name.

But there is another spiritual man, the one who has passed beyond the beginning and walks toward the inner way. Such believers withdraw into the inward parts of their spirits and there relinquish everything about themselves into the hands of God. They have forgotten and despoiled themselves of everything. And not only *things*, but *themselves*!

With an uplifted face and an uplifted soul, they come into the presence of their Lord. They come by faith. They come there without imagining what God is like nor forming some picture of Him. They come to Him with assurance—assurance that is found in tranquillity and in inward rest. They come, having collected their entire consciousness and centered all their being in one place—on Him.

You can be sure that such people have also passed through a great deal of tribulation, and all of that tribulation came to them because it was ordained by His hand.

In everything they have denied themselves.

True, they are still subject to temptation, but out of temptation and tribulation come infinite gain. It is God who fights the battle from within them.

There is no news that causes them to overabundantly rejoice nor is there any news that fills them with sadness.

Tribulation cannot unnerve them; yet they have a holy fear before the Lord, resting only in their communion of heart with Him.

Those who seek the Lord *externally* have to always *do* something...outward mortification, efforts at destroying certain weaknesses, battles with desires, or the acquiring of spiritual knowledge, scriptural information, etc. But whatever external efforts we employ to know God, these will produce little or nothing. We cannot do anything of ourselves. That is, nothing *except* things that are miserable.

But what of the *inward* way? The inward way is a centering of the whole being in a loving manner in the Divine presence. There, *the Lord* operates! It is by Him that virtue is established; it is by Him that desires are eradicated; it is by Him imperfections are destroyed.

The believer has entered into the chambers of his spirit and there he lives in spirit without those great efforts of struggling. He finds himself free. Freed from so many things which the external way simply can never release him from.

—MOLINOS

# CLEANSING THE SOUL

There are two ways for the soul to be cleansed. The first is through affliction, anguish, distress, and inward torment.

The second is through the fire of a burning love, a love impatient and hungry.

It is true that sometimes the Lord uses both of these ways to deal with our souls. *All* revelation and insight into God, all true experiential knowledge of God, *arises from suffering*, which is the truest proof of love.

Oh, how I hope and wish for you that you can understand the great good that comes from tribulation. Tribulation cleanses the soul. The cleansing of the soul through tribulation is what produces patience.

Within tribulation can come inflamed prayer.

In the midst of tribulation we can exercise the most sublime acts of love and charity. To rejoice in the midst of tribulation brings us near to God. It is tribulation which annihilates and refines. It is that which takes the earthen and transforms it to the heavenly. Out of the human it brings forth the divine...transforming one and bringing it to the other, uniting them with the Lord.

Oh Christian, if you would know how to be *constant* in the fire of tribulation and *quiet* in the fire of tribulation, to be washed with the waters of affliction, then you would discover just how soon divine goodness would make its throne in your soul. There, in that good habitation, God would be able to refresh and solace Himself.

—MOLINOS

# SOLITUDE

There are two kinds of solitude. There is an outward solitude when one simply does not speak, or speaks little.

There is also an inner solitude. Inner solitude means forgetting about everything around you, being detached from it, surrendering all purpose and desire and thought and will, and *then* coming before the Lord. This is true solitude. You will find it to be a sweet rest and an inward serenity...found in the arms of your Lord. For that believer who is able to stay in such a place before his Lord there will be a great number of discoveries.

For the believer who comes this far there is the discovery that the Lord converses and communicates with the believer in his inward parts. It is in *that* place the Lord fills the believer with Himself...but fills him only because that person is *empty*; He clothes him with light and with love because he is naked, lifts him up because he is lowly, and unites him with God and transforms him, because he is alone.

I see this solitude with God as a figure of eternal bliss—a picture of that future time when the eternal Father will be forever beheld.

—MOLINOS

# SIGNS OF THE INNER MAN

There are four signs by which you may know the inner man.

The first pertains to will and thought. The will is so trained that it engages in no act of love other than that which is toward God or pertaining to God and His purpose.

Secondly, when outward tasks are completed, the thoughts and will of the believer are quickly turned toward God.

Thirdly, if the believer enters into prayer, all other things are forgotten as if they had never been seen or known.

Fourthly, whereas the believer once feared the world, now he even fears the outward things of his own nature to the same degree he once feared the world. He shuns, therefore, not only the world, but outward things—except in those cases where charity requires outward performance.

Lastly, a believer who abides within the inmost portion of his being (within his spirit) lives in unbroken peace. Surely there may be outward combats, but the peace is not broken. There is an infinite distance between that inner place and the external tempest; the externals simply cannot reach this heavenly place. The believer can find himself even forsaken, opposed and desolate, but such a storm can only threaten and rage *without*. It has no power within.

—MOLINOS

# THE DEPTHS—EVEN
## FOR THE UNLEARNED

I would like to address this chapter to those of you who may not be able to read.[1] Because you cannot read, you may feel that you are in a weaker state than most Christians. You may feel you are unqualified to know the depths of your Lord. But in fact, you are really blessed. The blessing in not being able to read is that prayer may become your reading! Do you not know that the greatest book is *Jesus Christ* Himself? He is a Book who has been written on within and without. He will teach you all things. Read Him!

The first thing you must learn, dear friend, is that "the kingdom of God is within you" (Lk. 17:21b).

Never look for the kingdom anywhere but *there*, within. Once you have realized that the kingdom of God is within you and can be found there, just come to the Lord.

As you come, come with a deep sense of *love*; come to Him very *gently*; come to Him with a deep sense of *worship*. As you come to Him, humbly acknowledge that He is everything. Confess to Him that you are nothing.

Close your eyes to everything around you; begin to open the inward eyes of your soul, turning those eyes to your spirit.

91

In a word, give your full attention to the deep inward parts of your being.

You need only believe that God dwells in you. This belief, and this belief alone, will bring you into His holy presence. Do not allow your mind to wander about but hold it in submission as much as possible.

Once you are in the Lord's presence, be still and quiet before Him.

And now, there in His presence, simply begin to repeat the Lord's Prayer. Begin with the word, "Father." As you do, let the full meaning of that word deeply touch your heart. Believe that the God who lives inside you is indeed so willing to be your Father. Pour out your heart to Him as a little child pours out his heart to his father. *Never* doubt your Lord's deep love for you. *Never* doubt His desire to hear you. Call on His name and remain before Him silently for a little while. Remain there, waiting to have His heart made known to you.

As you come to Him, come as a weak child, one who is all soiled and badly bruised—a child that has been hurt from falling again and again. Come to the Lord as one who has no strength of his own; come to Him as one who has no power to cleanse himself. Humbly lay your pitiful condition before your Father's gaze.

—GUYON

# MEDITATING ON THE LORD'S PRAYER

While you wait there before Him, occasionally utter a word of love to Him and a word of grief over your sin. Then simply wait for a while. After waiting, you will sense when it is time to go on; when that moment comes, simply continue on in the Lord's Prayer.

As you speak the words, "Thy Kingdom come," call upon your Lord, the King of Glory, to reign in you.

Give yourself up to God. Give yourself to God so that *He* may do in your heart what you have so long been a failure in trying to do.

Acknowledge before Him His right to rule over you.

At some point in this encounter with your Lord, you will feel deep within your spirit that it is time to simply remain silent before Him. When you have such a sense, do not move on to the next word—not as long as this sense continues with you. You see, it is the Lord Himself who is holding you to silence. When that sense of waiting before Him has passed, go on again to the next words of the Lord's Prayer.

"Your will be done on earth as it is in heaven."

Praying these words, humble yourself before the Lord, earnestly asking Him to accomplish His whole will in you and through you. Surrender your heart into His hands. Surrender your freedom into His hands. Yield to your Lord His right to do with you as He pleases.

Do you know what God's will is?

His will is that His children love Him. Therefore, when you pray, "Lord, Your will be done," you are actually asking the Lord to allow you to *love* Him. So begin to love Him! And as you do, beseech Him to give you His love.

All that I have just described to you will take place very sweetly, and it will take place very peacefully, throughout the entire prayer.

—GUYON

# THE SECOND LEVEL

Now with these words behind us, let us look at this new level of prayer.

First of all, come into the Lord's presence by faith. As you are there before Him, keep turning inward to your spirit until your mind is collected and you are perfectly still before Him. Now, when all your attention is finally turned within and your mind is set on the Lord, simply remain quiet before Him for a little while.

Perhaps you will begin to enjoy a sense of the Lord's presence. If that is the case, *do not try to think* of anything. Do not try to *say* anything. Do not try to *do* anything! As long as the sense of the Lord's presence continues, *just remain there.* Remain before Him exactly as you are.

The awareness of His presence will eventually begin to decrease. When this happens, utter some words of love to the Lord or simply call on His name. Do this quietly and gently with a believing heart. In so doing, you will once again be brought back to the sweetness of His presence! You will discover that you once more return to that sweet place of utter enjoyment that you have just experienced! Once the sweetness of His presence has returned to its fullest, *again* be still before Him.

*You should not seek to move as long as He is near.*

What is the point? The point is this: There is a fire within you and it ebbs and grows. That fire, when it ebbs, must be gently fanned, but *only* gently. Just as soon as that fire begins to burn, again *cease all* your efforts. Otherwise, you might put out the flame.

94

This, then, is the second level of prayer—a second level in experiencing Jesus Christ.

When you have come to the end of this time, always remain there before the Lord, quietly, for a little while. Also, it is very important that all of your prayer be done with a believing heart. Praying with a believing heart is more important than *anything else* that has to do with prayer!

—GUYON

# PERIODS OF DRYNESS

Dear reader, you must realize that God has only one desire. Certainly you can never understand a dry spell unless you understand what His desire is. His desire is to give Himself to the soul that really loves Him and to that soul which earnestly seeks Him. *And yet* it is true that this God who desires to give Himself to you will often conceal Himself from you—from you, the very one who seeks Him!

Now why would God do that? Dear saint of God, you must learn the ways of your Lord. Yours is a God who often hides Himself. He hides Himself for a purpose. Why? *His purpose is to rouse you from spiritual laziness.* His purpose in removing Himself from you is to cause you to pursue Him.

The Lord Jesus is looking about everywhere for that Christian who will remain faithful and loving even when He has withdrawn Himself. If the Lord finds such a faithful soul, when He does return, He rewards the faithfulness of His child. He pours out upon that faithful one abundant goodness and tender caresses of love.

Here, then, is something you must understand.

You *will* have times of spiritual dryness. It is part of the Lord's way.

But the fact you will have spiritual dry spells is *not* the issue. The important question is what you will *do* in a time of spiritual dryness? At this point you must learn something about your natural tendencies. It will be the natural thing for you, during a dry season, to try to *prove* your love to the Lord. During a spiritually dry season you will find that you will try to prove to the Lord your faithfulness toward Him; you will do this by exerting your strength. Unconsciously you will be hoping by such self-effort to persuade Him to return more quickly.

No, dear Christian, believe me, this is not the way to respond to your Lord in seasons of dryness.

What then shall you do?

You must await the return of your Beloved with *patient love*. Join with that love *self-denial* and *humiliation*! Even though the Lord has hidden Himself, remain constantly before Him. There before Him, pour out your love upon Him passionately and yet, I would add, always peacefully.

Spend time with Him in worship and in respectful silence.

—GUYON

# LIVING INDOORS

How can we speak of a total victory over the five senses and over the passions and desire that become aroused through them?

If your body were dead, you would not be able to feel, and you certainly would have no desire. But why? Why would the body have no desire? Because it would be disconnected from the soul. So let me repeat, your feelings and your senses draw their power from the soul.

Christians have sought to find many ways to overcome their desires. Perhaps the most common approach has been discipline and self-denial. But no matter how severe your self-denial may be, it will never completely conquer your senses.

No, self-denial is not the answer!

Even when it appears to have worked, what self-denial has actually done is to change only the *outward expression* of those desires.

When you deal with the externals, what you are really doing is driving your soul farther outward from your spirit. The more your soul is focused on these outward things, the farther it is removed from its center and from its resting place! The result of this type of self-denial is the opposite of what you sought. Unfortunately, this is what always happens to a believer when his life is lived out on the surface.

If you dwell on the desires of your outward nature—paying attention to them—they, in turn, become more and more active. Instead of being subdued, they gain more power. We can conclude from all this that although self-denial may truly weaken the body, it can *never* take away the keenness of your senses.

Then what is your hope?

There is only one way to conquer your five senses, and that is by inward recollection. Or, to put it another way, the only way to conquer your five senses is by turning your soul completely inward to your spirit, there to possess a *present*

God. Your soul must turn all of its attention and energies *within*, not without! Within to Christ, not without to the senses. When your soul is turned within, it actually becomes *separated* from you external senses; and once your five senses are separated from your soul, they receive no more attention. Their life supply is cut off!

They become powerless.

Now let us follow the course of the soul. Your soul has learned at this point to turn within and draw near to the presence of God. The soul becomes farther and farther separated from the self. You may experience being powerfully drawn within—to seek God in your spirit—and discover that the outer man becomes very weak. (Some may even be prone to faintings.)

Your main concern, therefore, is with the presence of Jesus Christ. Your main concern lies in dwelling continually upon the God who is within you. Then, without particularly thinking of self-denial or "putting away the deeds of the flesh," God will cause you to experience a natural subduing of the flesh! You can be sure of this: The Christian who has faithfully abandoned himself to the Lord will soon discover that he also has laid hold of a God who will not rest until *He* has subdued everything! Your Lord will put to death all that remains to be put to death in your life.

What, then, is required of you? All you need to do is remain steadfast in giving your utmost attention to God. *He* will do all things perfectly. The truth is, not everyone is capable of severe outward self-denial, but *everyone* is capable of turning within and abandoning himself wholly to God.

—GUYON

# Toward the Center

As you come into this deeper level of knowing the Lord, you will eventually come to discover a principle I will call the *law of central tendency.*

What do I mean by the law of central tendency? As you continue holding your soul deep in your inward parts, you will discover that God has a *magnetic* attracting quality! Your God is like a magnet! The Lord naturally draws you more and more toward Himself.

The next thing you notice is this: As you move toward the center, the Lord also *purifies* you of all the things that are not of Him.

This is illustrated in nature. Observe the ocean. The water in the ocean begins to evaporate. Then the vapor begins moving toward the sun. As the vapor leaves the earth, it is full of impurities; however, as it ascends, it becomes more refined and more purified.

What did the vapor do?

The vapor did nothing. It simply *remained passive.* The purifying took place as the vapor was drawn up into the heavens!

There is one difference between your soul and those vapors. Although the vapor can *only* be passive, you have the privilege of cooperating *voluntarily* with the Lord as He draws you inwardly toward Himself.

When your soul is once turned toward God—the God who dwells within your spirit—you will find it easy to keep turning within. The longer you continue to turn within, the closer you will come to God and the more firmly you will cling to Him.

Of course, the closer you are drawn to God, the farther you are removed from the activities of your natural man. The natural man, to be sure, is very opposed to your inward drawing toward God. Nonetheless, there will come a point when you will finally be established in having turned within. From that point on, it will be natural for you to live before the Lord! In the past it was natural for you to live on the *surface* of your being; now it will be your habit to live in the *center* of your being where your Lord dwells.

—GUYON

# SILENCE

The point to which this venture has led us is a *state of silence* and *continuous prayer.*

Let us go back a little and take a closer look at this matter of silence. Why, for instance, is being silent before the Lord when you first come to Him so important? First of all, it is because your fallen nature is opposed to God's nature. The two are not at all alike. Secondly, Jesus Christ is the Word, the *speaking* Word. He can speak. He can be heard! But for the Word (Jesus Christ) to be received by you, *your* nature must be made to correspond to His nature.

Let me illustrate further.

Consider the act of hearing. Listening is a *passive* sense. If you ever want to hear anything, you must yield a passive ear.

Jesus Christ is the Eternal Word. He, and He alone, is the source of new life to you. For you to have new life, He must be communicated to you. He can speak. He can communicate. He can impart new life. And when He desires to speak to you, He demands the most intense attention to His voice.

Now you can see why the Scripture so frequently urges you to listen, to be attentive to the voice of God.

*Hearken unto Me, My people; and give ear unto Me, O My nation* (Isaiah 51:4a).

*Hear Me, all you whom I carry in My bosom, and bear within My bowels.* (See Isaiah 46:3.)

*Hearken, oh daughter, and consider and incline your ear; forget also your own people, and your father's house; so shall the king greatly desire your beauty.* (See Psalm 45:10-11a.)

Here is how to begin to acquire this habit of silence. First of all, forget yourself. That is, lay aside all self-interest.

Secondly, listen attentively to God.

These two simple actions will gradually begin to produce in you a love of that beauty which *is* the Lord Jesus! This beauty is inwrought in you *by* Him.

One other thing. Try to find a quiet place. Outward silence develops inward silence; and outward silence improves inward silence as it begins to take root in your life.

It is impossible for you to really become inward, that is, to live in your inmost being where Christ lives, without loving silence and retirement.

Hosea said it well:

*I will lead her into solitude, and there I will speak to her heart.* (See Hosea 2:14.)

You are to be completely occupied, inwardly, with God. Of course, this is impossible if, at the same time, you are outwardly busied with a thousand trifles.

The Lord is *at* the center of your being; therefore, He must *become* the center of your being.

What are you to do when you become drawn away from this God who is your center? No matter what it is that draws you away, whether weakness or lack of faith, you must immediately turn within once more.

Be ready to turn within, again and again, no matter how often you are drawn away. Be ready to repeat this turning just as often as distractions occur.

It is not enough to be turned inwardly to your Lord an hour or two each day. There is little value in being turned within to the Lord unless the end result is an anointing and a spirit of prayer which continues with you during the whole day.

—GUYON

# THE SCRIPTURE

Let us take the Scripture first. Is there a deeper use you can make of the Scripture than has been mentioned up until now?

Remember, please, from an earlier chapter, that reading the Scripture is a way *into* prayer. Remember, too, that what you *read* may become *prayer*. Is there yet more the Scripture can provide? Yes, you can use the Scripture in yet a more refined manner than has been mentioned before. Let us consider that way. I will give you a brief, practical description.

First, come before the Lord and begin to read. Stop reading just as soon as you feel yourself being drawn inwardly. Stop reading when you feel the Lord drawing you in your inward parts to Himself. Now, simply remain in stillness. Stay there for a while. Then, momentarily, proceed with your reading; but read only a little. Always cease reading each time you feel a divine attraction drawing you deeper within.

What can you expect beyond this state?

From time to time you will *begin* to touch a *state of inward silence.* What shall be your response to such an experience? One thing is this: No longer burden yourself with spoken prayer. (At this time, to pray out loud, or in any conventional way, would only draw you away from an inward experience and draw you back to an outward, surface prayer.)

You will be *attracted* to silence so there is no reason to force yourself to speak.

But if you do not speak, *what* shall you do? Nothing! Simply yield to the inward drawing! Yield to the wooing of your spirit. Your spirit is drawing you deeper within.

One other word.

In all your experience of Christ, it is wisest for you to stay away from any set form, or pattern, or way. Instead, *be wholly given up to the leading of the Holy Spirit.*

By following your spirit, every encounter you have with the Lord is one that is *perfect*...no matter what the encounter is like.

—GUYON

# PRAYER REQUESTS?

As you continue in this venture with Christ—this venture that began as a simple way of prayer—yet another experience may await you. It is this: Do not be too surprised if you find you are no longer able to offer up prayers of petition.

You may find that prayers of *request* become more difficult. Yes, it is true that in the past you offered up petitions and requests with complete ease. Until now, praying this way was never difficult. But in this new relationship with your Lord, it is the Spirit who prays! And as the Spirit prays, *He* helps your weakness. He is making intercession for you. And *He* is praying according to the will of God.

*For we do not know how to pray as we should; but the Spirit Himself intercedes for us with groanings too deep for words.* (See Romans 8:26.)

There is your will; there is God's will. There is your plan; there is God's plan. There is your prayer; there is *His* prayer. You must agree to *His* plans. He takes from you all your own workings so that *His* may be substituted in their place.

Therefore, yield.

Let God do in you what He will.

In His prayers, which *He* prays, there is also His will. Let *Him* pray. Give up your own prayers; give up your own desires and your own requests. Yes, you have a will; yes, you have desires and requests. Nevertheless, let Him have the will, the desire that is in the prayers *He* prays.

But this relationship goes even deeper.

In order for God to have that which is found in His prayer, then you, the one praying, must give up your attachment to everything. This means you must live a life *in which there is nothing you want*! Be attached to nothing, no matter how good it is or appears to be.

—GUYON

# CONSUMED

If I were to say to you that one of the great elements of prayer is deep, inward worship, I am sure you would agree. We would both concur that without a deep, inward worship of the Lord we simply would not have real prayer. *Real* prayer, of necessity, has worship as its central element.

But there is another element to prayer, just as central, just as essential, as worship. And it is right here that we come to the central issue of man with God; moreover, without this element there is no real prayer; without it there can be no plunging into the very depths of Jesus Christ. Without this element there is no real prayer, no entrance into the depths of Christ, and no way that God can bring you to the ends which He plans for you.

And what is this aspect of prayer?

The *giving up of self* is a necessary part of prayer and of experiencing the depths of Jesus Christ.

(So once more we have stepped beyond prayer. Real prayer demands of the one praying that he utterly abandon self. Moreover, God desires that such a state ultimately become yours at *all* times.)

It is the Apostle John who speaks of *prayer* as being an incense—an incense whose smoke ascends to God and is received by Him.

*Unto the angel was given much incense, that he should offer it with the prayers of all the saints.* (See Revelation 8:3.)

As you come to the Lord, pour out your heart in the presence of God. Prayer *is* the outpouring of your heart to Him. "I...have poured out my soul before the Lord," said Hannah, the mother of Samuel (1 Sam. 1:15). This outpouring is an incense, and this incense is a total giving of your self to Him.

The incense offered by the wise men, laid at the feet of Christ in the stable of Bethlehem, is a picture of outpoured prayer to Him.

What is prayer? Prayer is a certain warmth of love. Ah, but more! Prayer is a melting! Prayer is a dissolving and an uplifting of the soul. This warmth of love, this melting, this dissolving and uplifting causes the soul to ascend to God.

As the soul is melted, sweet fragrances begin to rise from it. These fragrances pour forth from a consuming fire of love... and that love is in you. It is a consuming fire of love in your inmost being, a fire of love for God.

—GUYON

# ASCENT UNTO GOD

Now we must ask the central question: *How* does the soul ascend to God?

The soul ascends to God by giving up *self*, giving it up to the destroying power of divine love! Yes, giving up to the annihilating power of divine love!

This giving up of self is essential, absolutely essential, if you are to plumb, experience, and continually dwell in the depths of Jesus Christ. It is only by the destruction and annihilation of self that you can pay homage to the sovereignty of God!

You see,

The power of the Lord is great, and He is honored only by the humble. (Apocrypha)

Let us see if we can understand this just a little more clearly.

It is by the utter destruction of self that you acknowledge the supreme existence of God.

The hour must come when *you* cease *all* living in the realm of the self! You must *cease to exist in self* so that the Spirit of the Eternal Word may exist in you.

By the giving up of your own life, you make way for His coming! And it is in your dying that *He* lives!

Can this be made practical? Yes!

You must surrender your whole being to Jesus Christ, ceasing to live any longer in yourself, so that He may become your life.

*For you have died, and your life is hidden with Christ in God.* (See Colossians 3:3.)

Pass into Me all you who earnestly seek after Me. (Apocrypha)

But how do you pass into God! By *forsaking* your self that you may be lost in Him!

You can be lost in Him *only* by the annihilation of the self. And what has that to do with prayer? The annihilation of self *is* the true prayer of worship! It is a prayer you must learn— learn in all the totality of its deepest possible meaning. *This* is the experience that renders to God, and to God alone, all "blessing, honor, glory, and power, forever and ever" (see Rev. 5:13).

This experience, this prayer, is the *prayer of reality*. This is reality! Annihilation is worshiping God in spirit and in *reality* (see Jn. 4:23).

All true worship is "in spirit." To be "in spirit," the soul is annihilated. "In spirit" you enter into the purity of that Spirit that prays within you; you are drawn away from your own soulish and human methods of prayer. You are "in reality" because you are placed in the reality of the *all* of God and the *nothing* of man.

—GUYON

# SILENCE—IN THE DEPTHS

Let us go on now to the part silence plays in our advancing experience of Christ, for silence has a great deal to do with experiencing the Lord on a deeper plane.

On occasion some people have heard the term "the prayer of silence" and have concluded that the role the soul is to play in this prayer is one of dullness, deadness and inactivity. This, of course, is not the case. As a matter of fact, the soul plays a higher, more extensive role than in spoken prayer.

How is this possible?

The soul can be active and yet utterly silent. This is because it is the Lord Himself who has become the mover of the soul. The soul acts in response to the moving of *His* Spirit.

*For all who are being led by the Spirit, these are the sons of God.* (See Romans 8:14.)

Therefore, to engage in "the prayer of silence" does not mean that you cease all action. Instead, it means your soul acts by the moving of your spirit.

Perhaps Ezekiel can help us see this. Ezekiel had a vision of wheels. These wheels he saw had the living Spirit with them. Wherever the Spirit went, there the wheels went. If the Spirit stood still, the wheels stood still. If the Spirit ascended up from the earth into the heavens, the wheels rose up close beside.

The Spirit was in those wheels, and the wheels were moved by the Spirit. (See Ezekiel 1:19-21.) The soul is like those wheels. The soul can be active after its own things, or it can wait—wait until something deeper stirs. Then the soul becomes like those wheels, following the Spirit wherever it goes. The soul should, in the same way, yield to the leading of the living Spirit within. The soul should wait and be faithful to act *only* when the Spirit moves.

You can be sure that the Spirit *never* exalts the self-nature. (The soul, following its own inclination, so often does exalt the self.) What does the Spirit do? The Spirit moves forward, plunging toward the *ultimate* end. And what is that ultimate end? It is union with God.

Therefore, let the soul do nothing of itself in prayer. The soul must simply follow the Spirit until it reaches its ultimate end!

By this illustration I believe you can see that the soul does not cease all action. Its action is simply in perfect concert with the Spirit.

—GUYON

# PRAYER OF SILENCE

Let us go on now to consider "the prayer of silence" in a practical way. How do you begin to experience the Lord in an attitude of silence?

You see, when your soul is active on its own—that is, active *apart* from the activity of the Spirit—then by its very nature its activity is forced and strained! The soul's effort in prayer is *always* that of anxiety and striving.

This is actually to your advantage! You can easily distinguish when the soul is functioning!

Oh! All is so different when the soul is responding to the moving of the Spirit—responding to something far deeper within your being.

When the soul is responding to the Spirit, the action is free, easy and natural. It will seem that you are putting forth almost no effort at all.

*He brought me forth into a large place; He delivered me, because He delights in me.* (See Psalm 18:19.)

Once your soul has turned within and once your mind is set on the Spirit, from that moment on the inward attraction of the Lord's Spirit is very powerful. In fact, the attraction of your spirit toward the soul is stronger than any other force—

stronger than those things which would draw you back to the surface.

The truth is, nothing is as quick to return to its center as is the soul to the Spirit!

Is the soul active at this time? Yes! But the activity is so exalted, so natural, so peaceful, and so spontaneous that it will seem to you that your soul is making no effort at all!

Have you ever noticed that when a wheel rolls slowly, it is easy to see all of it. But as the wheel turns faster, you can distinguish very little. *This* is the soul at rest in God. When the soul is at rest in God, its activity is spiritual and very exalted. Nonetheless, the soul is engaging in *no* effort. It is full of peace.

Therefore, hold your soul at peace.

The more peaceful your soul is, the more quickly it is able to move toward God, its center.

—GUYON

## RESTORING THE SOUL

Yield yourself to the guidance of the Spirit of God. By continuing to depend upon His action, and not that action of the soul, the things you do will be of value to God. Only what you do in *this* way is of value to God and to His work on this earth.

Let us see this from God's point of view.

All things were made by the Word, and without Him was not anything made that was made. (See John 1:3.)

In the very beginning it was God who formed man by His Word. He made man in His own image. God was Spirit and He gave man a spirit so that He could come into him and mingle His own life with man's life.

This, of course, was the state of man before the Fall. At the time of the Fall, man's spirit was deadened. God lost His chance to move into man's spirit. Man lost the ability to contain the life of God and to bear the image of God.

It was very plain to see that if God were ever to restore man to what He intended him to be, man's spirit would *have* to be restored.

And how could God restore man's spirit? How could He restore the image of God in man?

By none less than Jesus Christ. It had to be the Lord Jesus Himself who gave life to man's spirit and restored the image of God. Why? Because Jesus Christ alone is the exact image of His Father. He alone brings the life of God into man.

No image can be repaired by its own efforts. The broken image has to remain passive under the hand of the workman.

What is your activity in this restoration? Your only activity should be to yield yourself completely to the inner workings of the Spirit. Jesus Christ has come into you, into your inmost parts. Yield to His workings there.

If a canvas is unsteady, the artist is unable to paint an accurate picture upon it. The same is true of you. Every movement of the self produces error. The activity of the self interrupts and defeats the design which Jesus Christ wishes to engrave upon you. You must, instead, simply remain at peace. Respond *only* to the Spirit's working.

Jesus Christ has life in Himself (see Jn. 5:26), and *He* must give life to every living thing.

This principle—the principle of utter dependence upon the Spirit and complete denial of the activity of the soul—can be seen in the church.

Look at the church. The Spirit of the church is a moving, life-giving Spirit. Is the church idle and barren and unfruitful? No! The church is *full* of activity. But her activity is this: complete dependence on God's Spirit. That Spirit moves her. That Spirit gives her life.

This principle functions in the church, and it is this principle which causes the church to be what she is. The exact same principle should operate in you! What is true of her should be true of her members. To be her spiritual children, you must be led by the Spirit.

The Spirit in you *is* active. The activity that is produced in your life as a result of following the Spirit is a much higher activity than any other.

(An activity is worthy of only as much praise as its source. An activity that comes as a result of following the Spirit is more praise-worthy than any other activity coming from any other source. Whatever is produced from God's Spirit is divine. Whatever comes from self, no matter how good it appears, is still only human, still only the self.)

Your Lord once declared that He alone has life. All other creatures have "borrowed" life. The Lord has life *in* Himself. That life, which is *in Him*, also carries with it *His* nature. This is the unique life which He desires to give to you. He wishes to give you divine life, and He wishes you to live by that life instead of the life of your soul. At the same time, you should make room for denying your soul, that is, denying the activity of your own life. The only way you can make room for the

113

life of God to dwell in you and to live in you is by losing your old Adam life and denying the activity of the self.

Why? Because this life you are receiving is the very life of God, the same life God lives by! Paul said,

*If any man be in Christ, he is a new creature; old things are passed away; behold, all things are become new!* (2 Corinthians 5:17)

But, and I repeat, the only way this becomes practical experience to you is by dying to yourself and to all your own activity so that the activity of God can be substituted in its place.

## Endnote

1. If you can read, don't skip this chapter because you will still be greatly helped! Please remember that until the last century a great majority of the world's population could not read. Jeanne Guyon has addressed herself to them. If this book is being read to one who cannot read, it will prove most helpful.

# STEPPING INTO HIS PRESENCE

# Turn Toward God

You need to take time to turn to God. Do not pray only when you have set aside time to do so. The busier you are, the more you must practice turning to God. If you wait until the time is convenient, there is little doubt that you will end up spending little time with God.

Try to come before God both in the morning and the evening. Pray during and between all your other jobs as much as you can. You cannot retire too much from the mindless chatter of the world. Learn to steal this time in little snatches, and you will find these moments the most precious part of your day.

You don't need much time to tell God that you love Him! Lift your heart to Him. Worship Him in the depths of your spirit. Offer Him what you do and what you suffer. Tell God the most important things that occur to you; tell Him what stands out to you as you read the Bible. Cling to your dearest Friend; live in Him with unbounded trust; speak to Him out of a heart full of love. As you learn to continually turn your spirit toward the loving presence of God within you, you will find yourself strengthened to do what is required of you. Here is the kingdom of God coming to life within.

These times of inward retirement are the only solution for your quick temper, critical nature, and impatience. Turning to God will help you, but you will need to do it frequently.

As God draws you to Himself, follow Him with complete trust. Love Him as you would wish to be loved. Does this sound extravagant? It is not giving Him too much. As He shows you new ways to love Him, then do so.

Speak and act without too much planning and self-examination. Set your eyes on God and you will feel less of a need to please others. The wonderful thing is that you may end up pleasing them more.

—FENELON

## LEAN TOWARD HIM

Try, without forcing yourself, to turn to God and touch Him as often as you can. Even when you want to touch the Lord and you are distracted, it is important to keep bringing yourself before Him. Do not wait for a perfectly quiet time when you can lock yourself in your room and be alone. You know how hard it is to find such a time. The very moment you feel drawn toward God is the moment to turn toward Him. Simply lean toward Him with a heart full of love and trust. Do this when you are driving or dressing or getting your hair done. Turn toward Him while you are eating or others are talking. When conversation becomes boring, during a business meeting, for instance, you can find a few moments to fellowship with your Father instead of being drained by unnecessary talk.

Be faithful to your times of prayer whether or not you find any comfort in them. Make use of the time during the day when you are only slightly busy. Occupy every spare second with God. Even when you are doing needlework you can be aware of God's presence. It is harder to be aware of His presence when you are engaged in a conversation, but you can learn to sense Him within you, monitoring your words, and restraining all outbreaks of pride, hatred, and self-love. Do your work steadily and reliably. Be patient with yourself.

Something else you should remember is to watch your actions and hold yourself back if you see yourself about to do something wrong. If you do something wrong, bear the humiliation of your error. But try to yield immediately to the warning the Holy Spirit is giving you within. Faults done in haste or because of human weakness are nothing compared to closing your ear to the inner voice of the Holy Spirit.

And if you do commit a sin, realize that getting upset and feeling sorry for yourself will do no good. Pick yourself up and go on without letting your pride get its feathers ruffled.

Admit you were wrong, ask forgiveness, then go on. Being irritated with yourself is not what it means to pick yourself up and go on in peace. Don't be so upset by your mistakes.

Often what you offer God is not what He wants. He usually wants that which you dread giving Him. It is Isaac, the well beloved, that He wants you to give up. What He is after is what comes between you and Him. He will not rest, and neither will you, I might add, until you have given Him everything. If you want to prosper and enjoy God's blessing, don't hold anything back from Him. What comfort, freedom, and strength there is when nothing stands between you and God.

—FENELON

# LISTEN TO GOD

Don't listen to your self-nature. Self-love whispers in one ear and God whispers in the other. The first is restless, bold, eager, and reckless; the other is simple, peaceful, and speaks but a few words in a mild, gentle voice. As soon as you listen to the loud voice of self you will not hear the soft tones of holy love. Each speaks only of one thing. Self-love speaks only of self—it never gets enough attention. Self-love talks of being well thought of. The self despairs of everything except downright flattery.

God's love, on the other hand, whispers that self should be forgotten—counted as nothing so that God might be all. God wants to completely fill you and unite Himself to you. Let the vain, complaining babble of self-love be silenced so that in the stillness of the heart you may listen to the love of God.

While you live on earth you can understand only in part. The self-love, which is the source of your faults, is also what hides your faults. Self-love must be rooted out of you so that God can reign within you without opposition.

The light of God will show you what you are really like, and will also heal you of your sins. Until you see yourself in God's pure light, you really don't know yourself. You really rely on yourself much more than you think.

God's love will cause you to see clearly that He loves you without partiality and without flattery. This is how you must see yourself, as well as your neighbor. But relax, God only shows you your weakness as He gives you the courage to bear the sight! You will be shown your imperfections one by one as you are able to face them. Unless God gives you grace to see your weaknesses, the knowledge of them would only lead to despair.

Those who correct others should watch for the Holy Spirit to go ahead of them and touch a person's heart. Learn to imitate Him who reproves gently. People do not need to see God condemning them, they must realize within themselves that they have done something wrong. Do not be heavy-handed lest people see God as a judgmental ogre. When you become outraged over a person's fault, it is generally not "righteous indignation" but your own impatient personality expressing itself. Here is the imperfect pointing a finger at the imperfect. The more you selfishly love yourself, the more critical you will be. Self-love cannot forgive the self-love it discovers in others. Nothing is so offensive to a haughty, conceited heart as the sight of another one.

God's love, however, is full of consideration, patience, and tenderness. It leads people out of their weakness and sin one step at a time. The less selfish you are, the more considerate you will be of others. Wait a long time, wait years, before giving advice. And then only give advice as God opens the hearts of those who are to receive it. If you pick fruit before the fruit ripens, you will spoil it completely.

Your imperfect friends, and we are all imperfect, can only know you imperfectly. They see in you what you cannot see and overlook much that you do see. They are quick to see things that offend them, but they do not look deep within to the faults that are deeply hidden. Even their best judgments are superficial.

Listen to the voice of God in silence. Be willing to accept what He wants to show you. God will show you everything you need to know. Be faithful to come before Him in silence.

When you hear the still, small voice within, it is time to be silent. This voice is not a stranger to your spirit. It is God's voice within your spirit. This is not something mystical but something practical. Deep within you will learn to yield to God and to trust your Lord.

—FENELON

# DEPEND ON GOD

The best place to be is where God puts you. Any other place is undesirable because you chose it for yourself. Do not think too much about the future. Worrying about things that haven't happened yet is unhealthy for you. God Himself will help you, day by day. There is no need to store things up for the future. Don't you believe that God will take care of you?

A life of faith does two things: Faith helps you see God behind everything that He uses. And faith also keeps you in a place where you are not sure what will happen next. To have faith you cannot always want to know what is happening or going to happen. God wants you to trust Him alone from minute to minute. The strength He gives you in one minute is not intended to carry you through the next. Let God take care of His business. Just be faithful to what God asks of you. To depend on God from moment to moment—especially when all is dark and uncertain—is a true dying to your old self. This process is so slow and inward that it is often hidden from you as well as others.

When God takes something away from you, you can be sure He knows how to replace it. There is a story that when

Paul was alone in the desert, a raven brought him half a loaf of bread every day. If Paul's faith wavered and he wanted to be sure to have enough, he might have prayed that the raven would bring enough for two days. Do you think the raven would have come back at all! Eat in peace what God gives you. "Tomorrow will take care of itself" (see Mt. 6:34). The One who feeds you today will surely feed you tomorrow.

—FENELON

# YIELD YOUR WILL

Love does not depend on your feeling. Your will is what God wants from you. Run your household in a godly way, raise your children properly, and give up empty pleasures. Seek to be simple, quiet, and humble. Let your life be hid with Christ in God. This is what God is after.

When God asks you for something, do not refuse Him. Learn to wait for God. Do not move until He directs you. Each day will bring its own problems. As you deal with them you will grow deeper and deeper in God.

Let your faith strengthen you. When you feel absolutely weak you will discover a strength that is not your own. You will know that the strength is not your own. And if you go astray for a little while, then you will learn humility as you return. Your Lord lives in the center of your spirit. Return to Him there as much as you can. Surrender yourself to God and learn to live by Him rather than out of your own strength. Little by little this learning to live by your Lord's strength unfolds within you. No longer will you cling to things that you can see, but you will cling to God, within you, and there you will find deep and true fellowship.

—FENELON

# WALK IN HIS PRESENCE

The heart of your life as a Christian is contained in God's words to Abraham, "Walk in My presence, and you will be perfect." God's presence calms your spirit, gives you restful sleep, and quiets your mind. But you must give yourself completely to Him.

It does not take much time to love God, to renew yourself in His presence and to adore Him in the depths of your heart. The kingdom of God is within you and nothing can disturb it.

When outward distractions and a wayward imagination hinder you from having a peaceful inner life, then you must, by an act of will, bring yourself before God. Not that you can force yourself into God's presence, but even the desire to come into God's presence is, in itself, a powerful aid to your spirit. Cultivate a pure and upright intention toward God.

From time to time you must stir up your deepest desires to be fully devoted to God. There need to be seasons when you think on Him alone, with a wholly undistracted love. Consecrate your senses to Him completely at these times. Don't get caught up with things that you know distract you both outwardly and inwardly from God. Once you are distracted from God it is hard to return to Him. Whenever you notice that you want anything too much, then stop yourself immediately. God does not dwell in the midst of chaos and disorder. Don't get caught up with what is said and done around you. You will be deeply disturbed if you do. Find out what God expects from you in any given situation and stick strictly to doing that. This will help you keep your inner spirit as free and peaceful as possible. Get rid of everything that hinders you from turning easily to God.

An excellent way to maintain a quiet spirit is to let go of every action just as soon as you complete it. Don't keep thinking about what you have or haven't done! And don't blame yourself for forgetting something, or for doing something you regret. You will be much happier if you keep your mind only on the tasks at hand. Think of something only when it is time to think of it. God will tell you when the time comes to deal with something. You will exhaust your mind by trying to figure out God's will before the right time comes.

Make a habit of bringing your attention back to God on a regular basis. You will then be able to quiet all your inner commotion as soon as it starts to be churned up. Cut yourself off from every pleasure that does not come from God. Seek God within, and you will undoubtedly find Him with peace and joy. Be more occupied with God than anything else. Do everything with the awareness that you are acting before God and for His sake. At the sight of God's majesty, calmness and well-being should fill your spirit. A word from the Lord stilled the raging sea and a glance from Him to you, and from you to Him, will do the same for you.

Lift up your heart to God. He will purify, enlighten, and direct you. David said, "I have set the Lord always before me." Repeat His beautiful words, "Whom have I in heaven but You, and there is none on earth I desire that compares with You."

Do not wait for the time when you can shut the door without interruption. The moment you long for inward prayer is enough to bring you into God's presence. Turn toward God simply, trustfully, and with familiarity. Even in those moments you are most interrupted, you can turn toward your Father. Instead of being annoyed by unprofitable talk, you can find relief in finding a moment of inward fellowship with God. So you see how all things work together for good to those that love God.

Read what is suited to your current needs. Pause, as you read, to listen to God's voice directing you. Two or three simple words, full of God's spirit, are like food for the spirit. The words are forgotten, but they are still doing their work secretly, and the spirit feeds on them and grows strong.

—FENELON

# REST IN GOD

Virtue starts to grow in a heart that desires the will of God. It is not a question of knowing a lot, or being talented, or even of doing great deeds. All that you really need is to long to belong completely to God. But how does your will come to this place? By conforming little by little, but without reservation, to what God wants. You must learn to bring your weak will in line with God's all-powerful one. Here you will find inexhaustible and never-ending peace and joy.

Adore, praise, and bless God for everything! See Him in all things. There is no longer anything truly evil in your life for God uses even the most terrible sufferings to work for your good because you love Him. Can the troubles God uses to purify your life be called evil? Think of what these troubles accomplish in your life.

Rest all your cares on the bosom of the Father. Be content to follow His will in all things, and to let Him bring your will into harmony and oneness with Him. Do not resist Him as He works within you. If you feel resistance rising up inside of you, turn to Him and take His side against your own rebellious nature. He will know what to do. Learn not to grieve the Holy Spirit within you, for He watches over your inner life. Learn from the past mistakes you have made without getting discouraged.

How can you better glorify God than by renouncing your own desires and letting Him do what pleases Him? He is truly your God when you see nothing but the hand of God ruling over all things in your life, and you worship Him with no outside pressure and even with no inward comfort.

To want to serve God in some conditions, but not others, is to serve Him in your own way. But to put no limits on your submission to God is truly dying to yourself. This is how to worship God!

Open yourself to God without measure. Let His life flow through you like a torrent. Fear nothing on the road you are walking. God will lead you by the hand. Let your love for Him cast out the fear you feel for yourself.

—FENELON

# SAY YES TO GOD

Becoming perfect is not becoming boring and strict like you think. What it demands is that you should be totally

127

devoted to God from the depths of your heart. When you are totally given to Him, then all that you do for Him becomes easy. Those who are completely God's are always content because they want only what God wants. In giving up things that displease God, you will find yourself a hundred times happier. You will know a clear conscience, a free heart, the sweetness of surrender to God, and the joy of seeing the light increase in your spirit. On top of this you will be delivered from the harsh dictatorship of your fears and from the evil desires of the world.

You may give up things, but it is for Him whom you love best. You may suffer but you will still be upheld deep within. And you will say a continued "yes" to all that God needs to do to conform you to His image.

God only wants one will between the two of you. Let yourself become soft in His hands. Are you afraid to give up your will to God? How blessed you will be to throw yourself into the arms of the "Father of mercies and the God of all comfort." What a mistake to fear giving yourself too completely to God. It only means that you are afraid of being too happy, of finding too much comfort in God's love, of bearing the Cross in your life too bravely!

Let go of the things of the earth so that you might belong completely to God. You need not give up everything entirely. When you already live a life before God, balanced with discipline, all you need is to let God's love direct and motivate you from within.

After your conversion, your position in life may not change although you will! Serve God in the place He has put you. So instead of being eaten up with pride and passion, you will live with freedom, courage, and hope. You will find that you can trust God, and you will look forward to eternity, making your current trials easier to bear. When earthly happiness slips away from you, God's love will give you wings to fly into His bosom, above all your troubles and cares.

—FENELON

# YOU ARE MADE FOR GOD

Everything is for God, and for His purpose. Of course He wants you to be happy, but that is not His highest aim. God's glory and His purpose are the end of all things. So seek out the eternal purpose of God and get in line with it. You will find happiness and salvation there, but not as an end in itself. It is all for God.

Not many people can even think of being all for God, and not for themselves, but this is the highest calling. It is hard to hear or understand this because you want to live for your own interests. And it is hard to convince a modern person that God is his final end, and that everything in life should be to God and for God. This doesn't mean that you can't enjoy yourself and your freedom in God. You must simply want God's purpose fulfilled more than anything else in creation. You belong to God, you have been made for Him. Your natural instincts tell you to protect your life, and take care of yourself. There is nothing wrong with this, but you can live by a deeper instinct within your spirit that lives only for God's glory.

Some people love God because in His goodness He reaches out to save them. But you can experience love for God even if He never reached out to save you (although this is an impossible supposition!). You can love God simply for who He is, and not for what He does for you. Do you see the difference? It is not wrong to be glad that God has saved you, it is simply better to not dwell on that, and to live for what God is really after in redeeming you.

If you think this kind of love is impossible, I have two things to say. Nothing is impossible with God. Are you going to accuse the greatest Christians of every generation to be living an illusion simply because you cannot match their standard?

Secondly, eternal life is a gift of God's grace. He is not obligated to give it to you, but He, nonetheless, has given His Son for you to inherit it. If, just for example, He chose to not give me eternal life, if at the moment of my physical death I disappeared into oblivion, then God and His purpose have not changed, have they? God was never obligated to save me, was He? Everything I have from Him, my life itself, is a gift of grace. Even if He chose to not save me for eternity, He is still my Creator, and is free to do with me what He wishes. God is still God. His character is still the same. His purpose remains unchanged. Shall I not still love Him for this?

But God has prepared you to be His forever. Dare you love Him too much? I will still love Him no matter what He does with me. Dare you love Him less, when He loves you more? Will the reward that awaits you make you more selfish? Is eternal life your goal, and not God Himself? Your love is weak indeed if this is true!

—FENELON

# KNOWING GOD

Most people don't really know God. They know what they have read, or been told, but it is an intellectual knowledge that lacks true spiritual experience. Most of us grow up being told there is a God, but I'm not sure how much we believe it. We don't act like we believe in God. And those who believe in God have a relationship based on fear rather than love.

How many love God and want to know Him for Himself? I pray there will always be such people even if they are rare. All of us were made for God. But when people are told to seek God within, it is like telling them to go to another planet. What is farther away and more unknown than the bottom of your own heart?

Oh God, we don't understand You. We don't know that we exist through You. Help me to see You everywhere. You allow an amazing thing: a mixture of good and evil in the hearts of even those who are most given to You. These weaknesses keep us humble and close to You. So choke back in my heart all that rises up to question Your goodness. Let me sit in silence before You, and then I will begin to understand. Nothing presses You to overwhelm Your enemies. "You are patient," says Augustine, "because You are eternal." Oh God, love Yourself in me. The more I love You, the more You pursue me with Your relentless love. Oh God, I adore You. You have made me for Yourself alone. I exist for You.

—FENELON

# LOVE GOD WHOLEHEARTEDLY

Dwell in peace. Your feelings of devotion to God and your enthusiasm to serve Him do not depend on your own ability. The only thing that you can control at all is your will. Give God your will without reservation. The important question is not "Do I enjoy being a Christian?" but rather, "Do I want what God wants?" Confess your faults. Do not be too attached to things of this world. Trust God. Love Him more than yourself. Love His glory more than your life. If you do not want these things, ask to want them. God will come to you with His love, and put His peace in your heart.

—FENELON

# An Inward, Invincible Fortress

Darkness, dryness, debilitating temptation—these are matters which God purges from the soul. First you should know that your spirit is the very center, the habitation, of the kingdom of God. (Your center is the Kingdom of God.) Your Lord reigns upon His throne, with rest, in that place. You will need to keep your heart in peace so that you may keep this inward temple of God a pure place.

Whatever the Lord sends into your life, there is no disturbance in that place.

For your good and for the profit of your spirit He will allow an envious enemy to trouble this city of rest, this throne of peace. Troubles will come to you in the form of temptations, tribulation, subtle suggestions. Anything and everything of God's creation may become involved in troubling you. There will be painful troubles and there will be grievous persecutions.

How are you to deal with such things? How can you be constant and cheered in your heart in the midst of all these tribulations? Enter into that inmost realm, for it is there you may overcome outward surroundings. Within you is a Divine fortress, and that Divine fortress defends, protects and fights for you.

—MOLINOS

# DIVINE LOVE

There is a fire of Divine love.

It is this love which burns the believer and can even cause the believer to suffer. How? Sometimes the absence of the Beloved greatly affects the believer.

Sometimes the believer hears the inward voice of the Beloved calling. It is as a gentle whisper and proceeds from out of the believer's inmost depths...where the Lord, the Lover, abides. It is this whisper which possesses the believer almost to the point of undoing. The believer realizes how near is his Lord and yet he also realizes how much of the soul has not yet been possessed by Him.

This intoxicates the believer and puts an insatiable longing within him to be changed into the likeness of his Lord. Therefore, it can be said of love: Divine love is as strong as death, for it kills just as surely as death kills.

—MOLINOS

# DRAWING INTO
# THE INNER CHAMBER

In seasons of desolation or in seasons of temptation, I would urge you to always learn to withdraw into the inmost chamber of your spirit. There, do nothing but behold God. It is in the depth of your spirit that is the place of true happiness. It is *there* that the Lord will show you wondrous things.

When we are therein engulfed and lose ourselves in the immeasurable sea of His infinite goodness and abide in it, steadfast and immovable, we have fulfilled our lot. There is found the reason for our existence.

It is to the believer who has, with humility and resignation, reached this deep place of seeking only to fulfill God's will, that the Divine and loving Spirit teaches all things with a sweet and life-giving function.

High and sovereign is the gift of that one who can suffer the cross both internally and externally with contentment and resignation.

What does it mean to be perfectly resigned? It means that the believer resolves to abide with God alone, esteeming with equal contempt those things called *gifts* and those things called *light* and *darkness*. The believer lives only in God and for Him.

Happy is the man who has no other thought but to die to his self-nature. Therein is a victory over the enemy. Yes, but there is also victory over self. In that victory you will find a pure and unadulterated love, and a perfect peace toward your Lord. The believer who leaves *all* to find the Lord begins to possess all for eternity.

There is a great difference which lies between this thing of *doing* and this thing of suffering and dying.

Doing is delightful. It belongs to beginners in Christ. Suffering belongs to those seeking. Dying—dying to the self—belongs to those who are being completed in Christ.

—MOLINOS

# COMING BEFORE HIM

The centermost part of your being, *there* is the *supreme region*. It is the sacred temple of the Spirit—the place where God delights to abide. It is there He manifests Himself to the one He created. He gives Himself in a way that transcends both senses and all human understanding.

It is in this place that the one true Spirit—who is God—dominates the soul and masters it, instilling into it His own enlightenment.

Do not misunderstand me; the highest place to which the soul can attain is a place of His will, a state of life composed more of the cross, patience, and suffering than it is of what men generally think of when they speak of *enjoyment*.

—MOLINOS

# THINGS THAT ARE SPIRITUALLY PLEASURABLE

The Christian may ascend to a divine interchange of love with the Lord by two methods. The first method is by sensible pleasure. The second is by heavenly desire.

The first is frail. The believer is so frail that he must be stirred to Christ by outward drawings of pleasurable love. His relationship with the Lord has its foundation resting mostly on those things which bring pleasure to the believer. Remove those spiritual pleasures and the believer is on a very shaky foundation. But the kingdom of heaven suffers violence, and is not conquered by the fainthearted.

The second ascent belongs more to heavenly places. I will speak of three stages of ascent.

The *first* stage is that of the believer's being filled with God and obtaining *a hatred for worldly things*. In this stage the Christian is satisfied only with Divine love and learns to be quiet in the presence of God.

The *second* stage is *inebriation*. This is when the soul has more than it can hold. Within this stage there is born within the believer a fullness of Divine love.

The *third* stage is *security*. Here all fear is cast out of the believer's soul, and in that empty place which is left by fear's departure comes a Divine love. The believer resigns himself to whatever it is that Divine pleasure decrees. And when I speak of resignation to the will of God I mean the believer would be willing to go to hell if he but knew that this was the will of the Most High. There is a sense, in this stage, that it is impossible to be separated from the Beloved and from His infinite treasure.

—MOLINOS

# TOWARD THE INWARD WAY

There are five steps toward the inward way.

The first is *enlightenment*. In this stage Divine affection is kindled. Divine love for Him dries up those things which are but human.

There follows, secondly, an inward *anointing*. Something like a liquid Spirit flows into the believer's being, teaches him, strengthens him and allows him to receive deeper understanding of the Lord and His way. With this comes a pleasure that seems heavenly.

The third stage is *growth* of the inward man, the spiritual man. As the inward man begins to grow stronger than the outer man a clear fountain of pure love for the Lord arises.

Next comes *illumination*. Illumination is something coming from the Spirit of God to the human spirit which dwells within the man.

At last, there is *peace*. Tranquillity. A victory over all fightings has come internally. Peace and joy are great. The believer seems to totally rest, as one abiding in Divine and loving arms.

By such do we ascend to the true Solomon.

—MOLINOS

# FOUR ASPECTS
# OF INTERNAL LOVE

The secret and internal love which the believer has toward his Lord and which the Lord has toward him has four aspects to it.

The first is illumination, which is an experiential knowledge of the greatness of God and an experiential knowledge of the believer's nothingness.

The second is an inflamed love, a desire to be consumed with Divine fire.

The third is a peaceful and joyful rest.

The fourth is an inward filling of the Lord's power. The believer is replenished and filled with God. The believer no longer seeks, desires or wills anything except the greatness and the infinite good which is his God.

There are two results that arise from these four aspects of love.

The first is a great courage to suffer for God. The second is a hope—even an assurance—that the believer can never lose God nor be separated from Him regardless of outward evidence.

—MOLINOS

# INTERNAL DISCOVERY

There are two things which lead to a knowledge of God. One is far away and the other one is near. The first is speculation. The other is internal discovery.

Those who seek after a great deal of knowledge and information about the ways of God are really trying to satisfy their reasonings and to attain to God by means other than those of the *spirituals*. In no such manner can you attain a true and passionate love for the Lord. Such men who seek after God by the acquisition of information about God and acquiring information about the Scriptures are really nothing more than scholars. They do not know the unseen realms, nor do they realize that hidden things of God are found only within the spirit. Nor have they come to touch those joys which abide in the inmost depths of the believer...that place where God keeps

His throne and communicates Himself to the one who comes and joins Him in that place.

Unbelievably, there are even some who condemn such a concept.

Why? Because they neither understand nor desire it. The theologian who does not find an internal way to his Lord misses that way because he is not seeking to enter by the gate which Paul speaks of when he says:

*If any man thinks he is wise among you in this world, let him become a fool that he may become wise.*

It has become a maxim among those who follow the internal way: *practice ought to be laid hold of before theory!*

This simply means that you should have some experiential exercise of having touched your Lord in a very real way before you start searching out knowledge and doing a great deal of inquiring about such matters.

—MOLINOS

# THINGS TO ABANDON

The men or women who would attain to that deeper walk with their Lord must abandon and be detached from these four things:

1. Creatures
2. Temporal things
3. The very gifts of the Holy Spirit
4. Self
5. And lastly, they must be lost in God.

This last one (5) is the most complete of all. Only the believer who knows how to be detached attains to being lost in God.

God is more satisfied with the affection of the heart than with worldly science and thought. It is one in a thousand who sees the heart cleansed of all that imprisons it and pollutes it.

It is purity of heart which is the chief means of attaining to Divine wisdom.

You will never reach the ways I have discussed here if you are not steadfast—steadfast especially in those times when God purges you. He will purge you not only of attachments to temporal and natural goods, but of your desire for knowing His sublime blessing and things that have to do with unseen realms; for it is upon these very things that the self-nature sometimes supports and feeds itself. Why is it that some people do all of the things that have been discussed here (and much more) and yet do not attain to an experiential knowledge of Divine encounter? It is because they do not subject and submit themselves wholly and entirely to God, who has light to give those who do. Nor do they deny, and allow to be conquered, their own self-nature. Nor do they give themselves totally to God with a perfect divesting of interest in themselves.

And finally, none of us as believers will be purified except in the fire of inward pain.

—MOLINOS

# GOD OR THE WORLD

All the basis for the loss of the self is founded in two principles. The *first* principle is to esteem yourself and things of the world very slightly. This means the renouncing of the self-nature, the forsaking of created things with holy resolution and energy.

The *second* principle is a great esteem for God. An esteem for Him that brings you to love Him, adore and follow Him without thought of personal interest even if that interest be very holy.

From these two principles will eventually arise conformity to the Divine will. This practical conformity to the Divine will—in all things—leads the believer to the death of the activities of the *self* and to a *will* that is in concert with God.

There must be no fixation on spiritual delights, nor even fixations on delights found in the unseen realms, and certainly not on emotions or affections. Such a road, if allowed, is filled with many illusions and disillusionments.

The proper path that you will take is one that includes the bearing of a very heavy cross. This road is the royal highway that leads to loss of self.

Can you understand that even honor and dignity and praise are matters that must be dealt with and put away? What place have these in your life? Would you compete with honor and praise that are for Him alone?

—MOLINOS

# A PRAYER

Oh, Divine Majesty, in whose presence the pillars of heaven do quake and tremble, You are more than infinite, and yet in your love the seraphim burn. Give me leave, oh Lord, to lament our blindness and ingratitude. We all live deceived, seeking this foolish world and forsaking You who are our God. We all forsake You, the fountain of living water, for the foul mire of the world.

Oh, children of men, how long shall we follow after vanity? What deception is it that causes us to forsake our Lord who is our greatest good? Who is it that speaks the highest truth to us and loves us most and defends us most? Where is there a more perfect friend or tender bridegroom or loving father?

Oh, Divine Lord, how few are those who are willing to suffer that they may follow Christ crucified, who embrace the cross. Oh, what a scarcity there is of those who are totally stripped, dead to themselves and alive to God and totally resigned to Your good pleasure.

—MOLINOS

# From the Shallows
# to the Depths

As you pick up this book, you may feel that you simply are not one of those people capable of a deep experience with Jesus Christ. Most Christians do not feel that *they* have been called to a deep, inward relationship to their Lord. But we have all been called to the depths of Christ just as surely as we have been called to salvation.

When I speak of this "deep, inward relationship to Jesus Christ," what do I mean? Actually, it is very simple. It is only the turning and yielding of your heart to the Lord. It is the expression of love within your heart for Him.

You will recall that Paul encourages us to "pray without ceasing" (1 Thess. 5:17). The Lord also invites us to "watch and pray" (Mk. 13:33, 37). It is apparent from these two verses, as well as many more, that we all live by this kind of experience, this *prayer*, just as we live by love.

Once the Lord spoke and said, "I counsel you to buy from me gold tried in the fire that you may be rich" (see Rev. 3:18). Dear reader, there is gold available to you. This gold is much more easily obtained than you could ever imagine. It is available to *you*. The purpose of this book is to launch you into this exploration and into this discovery.

I give you an invitation: If you are thirsty, come to the living waters. Do not waste your precious time digging wells that have no water in them. (See John 7:37; Jeremiah 2:13.)

If you are starving and can find nothing to satisfy your hunger, then come. Come, and you will be filled.

You who are poor, come.

You who are afflicted, come.

You who are weighted down with your load of wretchedness and your load of pain, come. You *will* be comforted!

You who are sick and need a physician, come. Don't hesitate because you have diseases. Come to your Lord and show Him all your diseases, and they will be healed!

Come!

Dear child of God, your Father has His arms of love open wide to you. Throw yourself into His arms. You who have strayed and wandered away as sheep, return to your Shepherd. You who are sinners, come to your Savior.

—GUYON

# PRAYER—KEY TO THE DEEP WAY

I especially address those of you who are very simple and you who are uneducated, even you who cannot read and write. You may think you are the one person *most* incapable of this abiding experience of Christ, this prayer of simplicity. You may think yourself the one farthest from a deep experience with the Lord; but, in fact, the Lord has *especially* chosen you! You are the one *most* suited to know Him well.

So let no one feel left out. Jesus Christ has called us all.

Oh, I suppose there is one group who is left out!

Do not come if you have no heart. You see, before you come, there is one thing you must do: You must first give your heart to the Lord.

"But I do not know how to give my heart to the Lord."

Well, in this little book you will learn what it means to give your heart to the Lord and how to make that gift to Him.

Let me ask you, then, do you desire to know the Lord in a deep way? God *has* made such an experience, such a walk, possible for you. He has made it possible through the grace He has given to all His redeemed children. He has done it by means of His Holy Spirit.

How then will you come to the Lord to know Him in such a deep way? Prayer is the key. But I have in mind a certain kind of prayer. It is a kind of prayer that is very simple and yet holds the key to perfection and goodness—things found only in God Himself. The type of prayer that I have in mind will deliver you from enslavement to every sin. It is a prayer that will release to you every Godly virtue.

You see, the only way to be perfect is to walk in the presence of God. The only way you can live in His presence in uninterrupted fellowship is by means of prayer, but a very special kind of prayer. It is a prayer that leads you into the presence of God and keeps you there at all times; a prayer that can be experienced under any conditions, any place, and any time.

Is there really such a prayer? Does such an experience with Christ truly exist?

Yes, there is such a prayer! A prayer that does not interfere with your outward activities or your daily routine.

There is a kind of prayer that can be practiced by kings, by priests, by soldiers, by laborers, by children, by women, and even by the sick.

May I hasten to say that the kind of prayer I am speaking of is not a prayer that comes from your mind. It is a prayer that begins in the heart. It does not come from your understanding or your thoughts. Prayer offered to the Lord from your mind simply would not be adequate. Why? Because your mind is very limited. The mind can pay attention to only one thing at a time. Prayer that comes out of the heart is not interrupted by thinking! I will go so far as to say that nothing can interrupt this prayer, *the prayer of simplicity.*

—GUYON

## LAUNCHING OUT

I would like to address you as though you were a beginner in Christ, one seeking to know Him. In so doing, let me suggest two ways for you to come to the Lord. I will call the first way "praying the Scripture"; the second way I will call "beholding the Lord" or "waiting in His presence."

"Praying the Scripture" is a unique way of dealing with the Scripture; it involves both reading and prayer.

Here is how you should begin.

Turn to the Scripture; choose some passage that is simple and fairly practical. Next, come to the Lord. Come quietly and humbly. There, before Him, read a small portion of the passage of Scripture you have opened to.

Be careful as you read. Take in fully, gently and carefully what you are reading. Taste it and digest it as you read.

In the past it may have been your habit, while reading, to move very quickly from one verse of Scripture to another until you had read the whole passage. Perhaps you were seeking to find the main point of the passage.

But in coming to the Lord by means of "praying the Scripture," you do not read quickly; you read very slowly. You do not move from one passage to another, not until you have *sensed* the very heart of what you have read.

You may then want to take that portion of Scripture that has touched you and turn it into prayer.

After you have sensed something of the passage and after you know that the essence of that portion has been extracted and all the deeper sense of it is gone, then, very slowly, gently, and in a calm manner begin to read the next portion of the passage. You will be surprised to find that when your time with the Lord has ended, you will have read very little, probably no more than half a page.

"Praying the Scripture" is not judged by *how much* you read but by the way in which you read.

If you read quickly, it will benefit you little. You will be like a bee that merely skims the surface of a flower. Instead, in this new way of reading with prayer, you must become as the bee who penetrates into the *depths* of the flower. You plunge deeply within to remove its deepest nectar.

Of course, there is a kind of reading the Scripture for scholarship and for study—but not here. That studious kind of reading will not help you when it comes to matters that are *divine!* To receive any deep, inward profit from the Scripture, you must read as I have described. Plunge into the very depths of the words you read until revelation, like a sweet aroma, breaks out upon you.

—GUYON

# BEHOLDING THE LORD

In "beholding the Lord," you come to the Lord in a totally different way. Perhaps at this point I need to share with you the greatest difficulty you will have in waiting upon the Lord. It has to do with your mind. The mind has a very strong tendency to stray away from the Lord. Therefore, as you come before the Lord to sit in His presence, beholding Him, make use of the Scripture *to quiet your mind.*

The way to do this is really quite simple.

First, read a passage of Scripture. Once you sense the Lord's presence, the content of what you have read is no longer important. The Scripture has served its purpose; it has quieted your mind; it has brought you to Him.

So that you can see this more clearly, let me describe the way in which you come to the Lord by the simple act of beholding Him and waiting upon Him.

You begin by setting aside a time to be with the Lord. When you do come to Him, come quietly. Turn your heart to the presence of God. How is this done? This, too, is quite simple. You turn to Him by *faith.* By faith you believe you have come into the presence of God.

Next, while you are before the Lord, begin to read some portion of Scripture.

As you read, *pause.*

The pause should be quite gentle. You have paused so that you may set your mind on the Spirit. You have set your mind *inwardly*—on Christ.

(You should always remember that you are not doing this to gain some understanding of what you have read; rather, you are reading in order to turn your mind from outward things to the deep parts of your being. You are not there to learn or to read, but you are there to experience the presence of your Lord!)

While you are before the Lord, hold your heart in His presence. How? This you also do by faith. Yes, by faith you can hold your heart in the Lord's presence. Now, waiting before Him, turn all your attention toward your spirit. Do not allow your mind to wander. If your mind begins to wander, just turn your attention back again to the inward parts of your being.

You will be free from wandering—free from any outward distractions—and you will be brought near to God.

(The Lord is found *only* within your spirit, in the recesses of your being, in the Holy of Holies; this is where He dwells. The Lord once promised to come and make His home within you (see Jn. 14:23). He promised to there meet those who worship Him and who do His will. The Lord *will* meet you in your spirit. It was St. Augustine who once said that he had lost much time in the beginning of his Christian experience by trying to find the Lord outwardly rather than by turning inwardly.)

Once your heart has been turned inwardly to the Lord, you will have an impression of His presence. You will be able to notice His presence more acutely because your outer senses have now become very calm and quiet. Your attention is no longer on outward things or on the surface thoughts of your mind; instead, sweetly and silently, your mind becomes occupied with what you have read and by that touch of His presence.

—GUYON

# ABANDONMENT

At the outset of this book we discussed how to know the depths of Jesus Christ. Our beginning was quite simple. We looked first at *praying the Scripture* and then at the simplicity of just *beholding the Lord*. After you have pursued this level of experience with the Lord for a *considerable* length of time, you then should be ready to go on to a deeper level of experience with Him and a deeper level of knowing Him. But in this deeper encounter with the Lord which we looked at in Chapter 4, you must move outside the realm of prayer alone; or, to state it more clearly, you must move away from just that one or two times a day you set apart for prayer with the Lord.

At this point, there must enter into your heart whole new attitudes toward your entire life. If you are to branch out beyond just a time of prayer each day, other parts of your life—and even your whole viewpoint of life—will have to be altered. This new attitude must come for a very special reason—so that you may go on deeper, still deeper, into another level with your Lord.

To do this, you must have a fresh attitude toward yourself as well as toward the Lord; it is an attitude that must go much deeper than any you have known previously.

To do this, I introduce a new word to you. The word is *abandonment*.

To penetrate deeper in the experience of Jesus Christ, it is required that you begin to abandon your whole existence, giving it up to God. Let us take the daily occurrences of life as an illustration. You must utterly believe that the circumstances of your life, that is, every minute of your life, as well as the whole course of your life—anything, yes, *everything* that happens—have all come to you by His will and by His permission. You must utterly believe that everything that has happened to you is from God and is exactly what you need.

Such an outlook towards your circumstances and such a look of faith towards your Lord will make you *content* with *everything*. Once you believe this, you will then begin to take everything that comes into your life as being from the hand of God, not from the hand of man.

—GUYON

# ABANDONMENT AND REVELATION

Some have asked the question, "If I utterly abandon myself to the Lord, will that mean I will have no new revelation of Jesus Christ?"

Does abandonment end revelation?

No, it does not. Quite the contrary, abandonment is the means that the Lord will use to give you revelation. The revelation you receive will come to you as *reality* rather than *knowledge*. This is made possible only by abandonment.

You must remember *to whom* it is you are abandoning yourself.

It is to the Lord Jesus that you abandon yourself. It is also the Lord whom you will follow as the Way; it is this Lord that you will hear as the Truth, and it is from this Lord that you will receive Life. (See John 14:6.) If you follow Him as the Way, you will hear Him as the Truth, and He will bring life to you as the Life.

As revelation comes to you, something happens; Jesus Christ actually makes an imprint of Himself upon your soul. Each time He comes to you, He leaves a new and different impression of His nature upon you.

Soon there are many different expressions of His nature impressed into your being.

Perhaps you have heard that you should *think* on the different experiences of Jesus Christ. But it is far better for you to bear, to carry, these experiences of Jesus Christ *within* yourself.

This is the way it was in the life of Paul. He did not ponder the sufferings of Christ; he did not consider the marks of suffering on the Lord's body. Instead, Paul bore in his own body the experiences of his Lord. He even said, "I bear in my body the marks of Jesus Christ" (see Gal. 6:17). Did he do so by considering such marks? No. Jesus Christ had personally imprinted Himself upon Paul.

When the Lord finds a believer who is completely abandoned to Him in all things *without* and in all things *within*, He will often choose to give that person special revelations of His nature. If such should be your experience, accept these revelations with a thankful heart.

Always receive everything from Him with a thankful heart, no matter what it is He chooses to bestow.

—GUYON

# CONTINUAL PRAYER

If you remain faithful in the things touched on up until now, you will be astonished to feel the Lord gradually taking possession of your whole being. I would like to remind you that this book was not written for your enjoyment. Neither is it presenting just some method of prayer. The purpose of this book is to offer a way in which the Lord Jesus *can take full possession of you.*

As the Lord gradually begins to do this, to take full possession of you, it is true that you will begin to enjoy a sense of His presence. You will find that this sense of the Lord's presence will become very natural to you. Both the prayer with which you first began and a sense of His presence *which comes with that prayer*, will eventually become a normal part of your daily experience.

An unusual serenity and peacefulness will gradually spread over your soul. Your whole prayer, your whole experience, will begin to enter upon a new level.

What is this new level? It is prayer. Prayer that consists of silence. And while in this silence, God pours into you a deep, inward love. This experience of love is one that will fill and permeate your whole being. There is no way to describe this experience, this encounter. I would only say that this love which the Lord pours into your depths is the beginning of an indescribable blessedness.

I wish it were possible in this little book to tell you some of the levels of endless experiences you can have with the Lord, experiences that come out of this encounter with God. But I must remember that this little book is written for beginners.

Therefore, I trust on some future day I will be able to relate these deeper experiences to you.

There is one thing I will say, however. When you come to the Lord, gradually learn to have a quiet mind before Him. One of the most important things you can do is cease from any self-effort. In this way, God Himself can act alone. It was the Psalmist speaking for the Lord who said, "Be still and know that I am God" (Ps. 46:10).

This verse gives you an insight into your own mind. Your self-nature becomes so pleasantly attached to its own efforts that it simply cannot believe that anything is going on within your spirit. Unless the mind is able to feel and understand, it refuses to believe the spirit is having experience.

The reason you are sometimes unable to *feel* God's working within you is that the work is fully within the realm of the spirit, and not in the mind. Sometimes God's workings in you are quite rapid, and yet the mind is not even aware that you are making progress. The workings of God in you, always increasing more and more, are absorbing the workings of your self.

—GUYON

# STILLING THE SOUL

You see, there are two kinds of people who keep silent. The first is one who has nothing to say, and the other is one who has too much to say. In the case of this deeper encounter with the Lord, the latter is true. Silence is produced from excess, not from lack. To die of thirst is one thing; to be

155

drowned is quite another. Yet water causes both. In one, it is a lack of water, and in the other, too much water causes death.

This experience with Christ has its beginning in a simple way to pray. Gradually, though, it goes on from there. The experience deepens until the fullness of grace completely stills the activity of the self. Therefore, you see why it is of the greatest importance that you remain as quieted as possible.

May I illustrate this again? When a baby is born, it draws milk from its mother's breast by moving its lips. However, once the milk begins to flow, the child simply swallows without any further effort. If the baby continued any effort, it would hurt itself, spill the milk, and have to quit nursing.

This must be your attitude in prayer. You must act this same way, especially in the beginning. Draw ever so gently. But as the Lord flows out of your spirit into your soul, cease all activity. How do you begin? By moving your lips, by stirring up the affections of your love for the Lord. As soon as the milk of divine love is flowing freely, be still—do nothing. Rather, very simply and sweetly, take in that grace and love. When this grace, this sense of the Lord's love, ceases to flow, it is time once again to stir up your affections. How? Just as the infant does by moving its lips.

All this time remain very quiet. If you bring yourself to the Lord in some other way, you will not make the best use of this grace. You see, the sense of the Lord's presence has been given to you, by the Lord, to allure you into a restful experience of love. It goes without saying that His presence has not been given to you to stir up an activity of the self.

—GUYON

156

# ABUNDANCE

At the very outset of this journey, you found that the only preparation you needed was a quiet waiting before God. The same is true in this new level of experience. This is no longer a rare experience, nor an occasional experience; gradually it becomes your *daily* experience. The presence of God begins to be poured forth within you. Eventually it will become yours almost without intermission.

In the beginning, you were led into His presence by prayer; but now, as *prayer* continues the prayer actually *becomes* His presence. In fact, we can no longer say that it is prayer that continues. It is actually His presence that continues with you. This is beyond prayer. Now a heavenly blessedness is yours. You begin to discover that God is more intimately present to you than you are to yourself, and a great awareness of the Lord begins to come to you.

I have said previously about each one of these experiences with the Lord, that the only way to find Him is by turning within. It is there, and there alone, you can find Him. Now you will discover that as soon as you close your eyes, you are enveloped in prayer. You will be amazed that He has blessed you so much.

It is at this point, therefore, that it is proper to introduce to you yet another experience; one that takes place deep within you.

There is born within you an internal conversation with God.

This conversation is highly enjoyable, and the most amazing thing about it is that no outward circumstances can interrupt it.

Now you see just how far that simple prayer you began with can lead you! The same thing can be said of the "prayer of simplicity" that was said of wisdom: "All good things come together in her." (Apocrypha)

And the same can be said of this deeper experience with the Lord. Godliness flows so sweetly and so easily from within the believer who has advanced this far that it even seems to be his very nature that pours itself out with such sweetness and ease. The spring of living water within the spirit breaks forth abundantly, producing every kind of goodness.

—GUYON

**OTHER BOOKS BY GENE EDWARDS**

**INTRODUCTION TO THE DEEPER CHRISTIAN LIFE**
*Living by the Highest Life*
*The Secret to the Christian Life*
*The Inward Journey*

**THE FIRST-CENTURY DIARIES**
*The Silas Diary*
*The Titus Diary*
*The Timothy Diary*
*The Priscilla Diary*
*The Gauis Diary*

**THE CHRONICLES OF THE DOOR**
*The Beginning*
*The Escape*
*The Birth*
*The Triumph*
*The Return*

**HEALING AND COMFORT**
*The Prisoner in the Third Cell*
*Exquisite Agony*
(Formerly titled Crucified by Christians)
*Letters to a Devastated Christian*
*Dear Lillian*

**TWO OF THE GREAT CHRISTIAN CLASSICS OF ALL TIMES**
*The Divine Romance*
*A Tale of Three Kings*

**You may contact the author at:**
Gene Edwards
P.O. Box 3450
Jacksonville, FL 32206
1-800-827-9825

Additional copies of this book and other book titles from DESTINY IMAGE are available at your local bookstore.

For a complete list of our titles, visit us at www.destinyimage.com Send a request for a catalog to:

## Destiny Image® Publishers, Inc.

P.O. Box 310
Shippensburg, PA 17257-0310

*"Speaking to the Purposes of God for This Generation and for the Generations to Come"*